CASSELL'S TECHNICAL CRAFT SERIES

Motor Vehicl Technology

GW00367243

W. A. Livesey

B.Ed.(Hons), T.Eng.(CEI), MIMI, MSAET, AIED

Lecturer in Motor Vehicle Studies
at Strode College, Street, Somerset

Cassell

London

Contents

CASSELL LTD

1 St. Anne's Road, Eastbourne, East Sussex BN21 3UN

© Cassell Ltd. 1983

First published 1983

British Library Cataloguing in Publication Data

Livesey, W.A.
  Motor vehicle technology—(Cassell's technical craft series)
  1. Automobiles—Design and construction
  I. Title
  629.2   TL145

ISBN 0-304-30427-1

Printed and bound in Great Britain by Collins, Glasgow

Preface

The author realises that the apprentice or other new recruit to motor vehicle work needs a textbook which sets down essential basic information in a clear and simple way. In following the City and Guilds 381 syllabus — Motor Vehicle Craft Studies — I have attempted to meet that need.

This book is particularly suitable for anyone studying towards the City and Guilds 381 examinations, the various regional boards, or the IMI. It will also be useful for anyone pursuing a training course in motor vehicle work, or those who just want to know about motor cars.

February 1983   Andrew Livesey

Acknowledgements
The author and publishers would like to thank the following firms and organisations who kindly supplied photographs for inclusion in this book: Austin Rover Group Limited, British Leyland (Austin Morris) Limited, Dunlop Limited, Fiat Auto (U.K.) Limited, Ford Motor Company Limited, Volvo Concessionaires Limited.

The cover shows a socket set which was kindly supplied by Snap-on Tools Ltd.
The photograph was taken by Andrew Watson.

Abbreviations

Abbreviations and SI units

Although the abbreviations used in this book are introduced with the appropriate terms, the student will no doubt find this list useful for quick reference.

Abbreviations

ABDC	after bottom dead-centre
ATDC	after top dead-centre
BBDC	before bottom dead-centre
BDC	bottom dead-centre
BTDC	before top dead-centre
CI	compression ignition
FWD	front wheel drive
IRS	independent rear suspension
kph	kilometres per hour
mpg	miles per gallon
mph	miles per hour
OHV	overhead valve
OHC	overhead cam
psi	pounds per square inch
RD	relative density
rpm	revolutions per minute
RWD	rear wheel drive
SAE	Society of Automotive Engineers
SI	spark ignition
TDC	top dead-centre

SI units

m	metre
km	kilometre
cm	centimetre
mm	millimetre
kg	kilogram
Pa	pascal
kPa	kilopascal
kV	kilovolt
N	newton
l	litre

1 The body and chassis

Vehicle layout

The chassis forms the backbone of the motor car and the body the covering around which the rest of the car is built, i.e. most of the components are designed to fit the size of car chosen. The layout of a car varies, depends upon its purpose and the manufacturer's particular design. There are three different classifications of vehicle layout: conventional, front-wheel drive and rear-wheel drive. We will study each in turn.

Conventional layout

Conventional layout is so called because it was originally the most popular design. The illustration shows an example of a conventional layout. As can be seen, the engine, which is the source of power, is at the front of the car, driving the rear wheels through the transmission system: clutch, gearbox, propeller-shaft and rear axle unit.

In a conventional layout the engine is mounted on the chassis at the front of the car underneath the bonnet. The cooling radiator and fan are mounted in front of the engine so that they are presented to the airstream as the car moves along, so aiding cooling of the engine. Behind the engine is the clutch. This allows the drive to the gearbox to be engaged or disengaged when changing gear or starting off from rest. The gearbox is attached to the bell-housing which contains the clutch and is supported at its rear on a rubber mounting to the chassis in the same way as the engine. The gearbox allows the ratio of engine speed to wheel speed to be varied. The propeller-shaft is splined or bolted to the gearbox main shaft. This transmits the drive from the gearbox to the flange on the rear axle. The rear axle carries the final drive gears, the differential and the rear road wheels, which both support

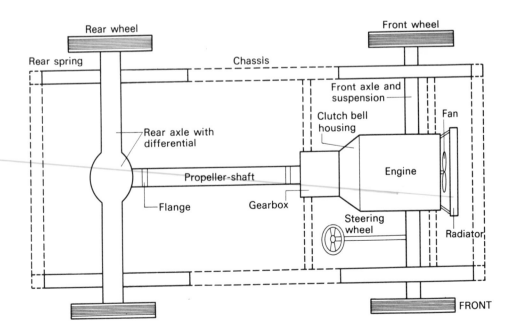

Conventional vehicle layout

and drive the car. The final drive gears turn the drive through 90 degrees. The differential allows the outer wheel to travel faster than the inner wheel when cornering. The rear axle is attached to the chassis by road springs.

The front suspension and the steering are attached to the front of the car with rubber bushes. The suspension mechanism pivots so that the car can be steered. The front road wheels, which are used to steer the car, are carried on the front hubs.

Front-wheel drive layout (FWD)

The majority of cars produced by the major motor manufacturers are now of the front engine, front-wheel drive type. As its name implies, the engine is mounted at the front and it drives the front wheels. The illustration shows the layout. With this arrangement the engine, the clutch, the gearbox and the differential are combined into one large unit, sometimes called the *power unit*. This complete

power unit is mounted onto the front of the chassis with rubber mounting blocks.

Drive from the power unit is transmitted to the front hubs through drive shafts. On front-wheel drive cars the front wheels both drive and steer the car. The rear wheels simply support the car through the rear suspension. The power unit may be fitted so that the cylinders and the crankshaft share the same axis with the chassis. When the engine is mounted in line with the chassis, as with a conventional layout, it is called *longitudinal mounting*. Where the engine is mounted longitudinally the radiator is usually at the front.

Alternatively, the power unit may be mounted so that the axis of its cylinders and crankshafts are at right-angles to the chassis. This is called *transverse mounting* (sometimes referred to as east–west layout). The radiator may be mounted at the front of the car, i.e. at the side of the engine. The layout shown in the illustration has a transverse-mounted engine.

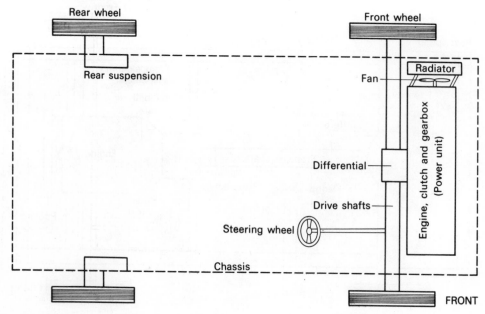

Front-wheel drive layout (transverse-mounted engine)

Rear-wheel drive layout (RWD)

The rear-wheel drive layout is called rear-engine rear-wheel drive. As its name implies, the engine is mounted at the rear of the car and drives the rear wheels.

Normally, in rear-wheel drive layouts the engine is mounted longitudinally, with the front of the engine at the rear of the car, as in the diagram. The radiator can be at the front of the engine, i.e. the extreme rear of the car, or at the side of the engine and car. The engine is fitted to the transmission through the clutch unit in its bell-housing. The bell-housing is incorporated into the transmission housing.

Most rear-engined cars have the gearbox, final drive gears and differential in one unit, which is called the *transmission unit*. The drive from the transmission unit to the rear wheels is through two drive shafts. The engine and the transmission are rubber-mounted to the chassis. The front suspension supports and steers the car.

Examples

Examples of popular cars with the different layouts mentioned above are given in the following table.

Conventional	Front-wheel drive	Rear-wheel drive
Morris Marina	Leyland Mini	Hillman Imp
Ford Cortina	Austin Allegro	Fiat 600
Vauxhall Viva	Austin 1100/	Volkswagen
Datsun Sunny	1300/1800	Beetle
Toyota Corolla	Austin Princess	
	Ford Fiesta	
	Renault 16	

Advantages and disadvantages

Each type of vehicle layout has certain advantages and certain disadvantages.

Space

The front-wheel drive layout has the most space for a given length of car. The power unit takes up the rather limited space between the front wheels and the passenger compartment has a large amount of space, depending on the given size of car. It also has

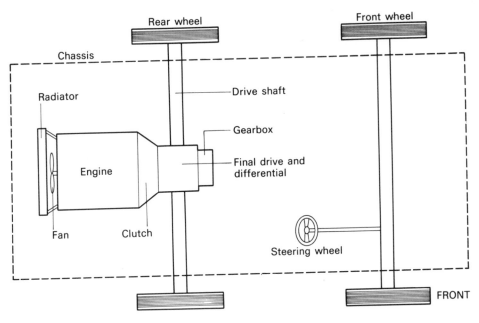

Rear-wheel drive layout

a flat floor. A rear-mounted engine and transmission will take up some of the car's length. The size of the luggage compartment, or boot, is restricted to the limited space above the steering suspension between the front wheels. The conventional layout offers the least amount of passenger space. The gearbox and the propeller-shaft project into the passenger compartment and the floor is shaped to allow these components to function.

Noise
The rear-engined car layout is the quietest of all to travel in, as all the noise is forced out behind the passenger seat. The conventional layout is noisy to a certain extent. The FWD is the noisiest of all, as all the rotating mechanical components are in front of the passengers.

Handling and traction
The FWD and the RWD cars have the best grip on the road, as the weight of the engine and transmission is over the driving wheels.

However, the position of these components affects the handling of the car, which does not happen with the conventional layout.

Mechanics and maintenance
The conventional layout is the simplest for maintenance, having the least complicated parts and the easiest accessibility to them. For any large mechanical repairs FWD and RWD cars generally need the power unit removed. RWD vehicles require long control rods and cables for the accelerator, clutch and gear change, as there is sometimes more than two metres between the driver and the power unit.

Safety
In a conventional layout vehicle the arrangement of the units is such that they can survive in a collision, whereas FWD vehicles are liable to mechanical damage. RWD vehicles have their petrol tanks mounted at the front. In a collision petrol is liable to be spilled over the vehicle, so increasing the risk of fire.

Types of chassis

Vehicles can be fitted with separate chassis, or the chassis can be integral with the body. There are three types of separate chassis in use: ladder, cruciform and backbone.

Ladder chassis
The ladder chassis is so called because it is shaped like a ladder (see illustration). There are two side-rails (A) connected by cross-members (B). The ladder chassis is used on many heavy vehicles as it can carry large loads. It is used on heavy cars, public service vehicles (PSV) and heavy goods vehicles (HGV). Although the ladder chassis can carry

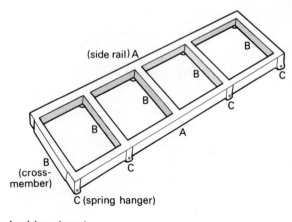

Ladder chassis

loads between the axles it is not strong in torsion, and it is easily lozenged if a corner is involved in a collision. The ladder chassis is flat, so the chassis is mounted high above the road to give the propeller-shaft and rear axle sufficient clearance for movement of the suspension. The suspension is connected by spring hangers (C) at each end of the leaf spring.

Cruciform chassis

The two centre-members of the chassis (B) form the shape of a cross. Hence the name cruciform (see illustration). The side rails (A) connect the components longitudinally and provide the mountings for the suspension and the body. The cruciform shape of the centre-members gives a high resistance to twisting, or torsional rigidity. Because of its shape, the cruciform chassis is economical in metal and therefore light in weight. It is used on light cars and sports cars.

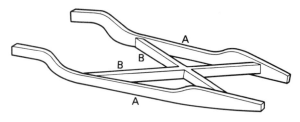

Cruciform chassis

Backbone chassis

The backbone chassis has a long central section to which are attached outriggers to the front and rear so that it looks like a human skeleton. The front outriggers carry the engine, the rear ones the rear axle. The central backbone section is hollow and is used to carry the gearbox and the propeller-shaft. The backbone chassis, like the cruciform chassis, is both light and torsionally rigid.

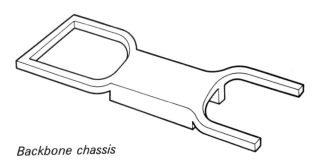

Backbone chassis

Body mountings

The traditional method of body-building is to use sheets of steel or aluminium on a frame of ash or similar wood. Modern bodies are made from a variety of materials such as pressed steel and glass-fibre.

The mounting of the body onto the chassis is done with rubber mountings to reduce the transmission of noise and vibration from the chassis to the body. The rubber flexes slightly. The mounting blocks are placed between the

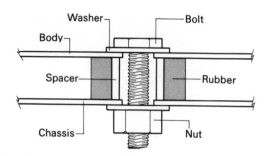

Body-chassis mounting

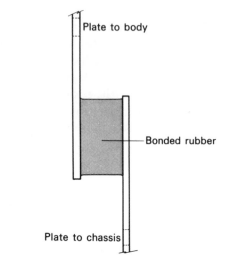

Body-chassis mounting

chassis and the body at strong points. The number of mounting points depends on the size of car and the type of mountings. The diagrams show some of the different types of mountings in use.

One type of mounting (body-chassis mounting) uses a rubber pad between the body and the chassis. To prevent the rubber from being squashed a spacer or a distance-piece is fitted between the two mating surfaces. Another type of body-chassis mounting has a piece of rubber sandwiched between two plates. The rubber is bonded to the two metal plates. The strength of the bonding supports the body on the chassis. These mountings are in shear.

Chassis section

Different shapes of chassis sections are used for vehicle chassis, and some examples are shown. The round section (a) is the strongest, followed closely by the square section (b). The square section has the advantages of being easier and cheaper to make and items can easily be screwed or welded to its flat sides. Where the loads are limited to one direction, or where strength is not a priority, the open-channel or U-section (c) is ideal. This is used on many chassis for outriggers and cross-members. L-section chassis members (d) are used where only a load support is needed, such as on trailers. I- or girder-section chassis (e) is used for special applications, for example as longitudinal runners on HGV chassis, especially trailers for articulated vehicles.

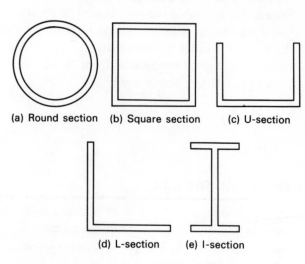

Chassis sections

Integral contruction

Integral contruction is also known as unitary contruction. This means that the body and the chassis are contructed as an integral unit, i.e. in one piece, not as two separate items. These are often referred to as body shells. The floor, the sills, the roof and the quarter panels are all welded together (usually spotwelded) to form a complete assembly to which the engine and the running gear can be attached. The integral body chassis is both stronger and lighter than the separate body-chassis contruction method.

Unitary construction

Types of bodies

There are many types of bodies in use. These are divided first into private and commercial vehicles then into more individual types of bodies.

Private vehicles	*Commercial vehicles*
Sports car	Small van, 250 – 350 kg (5 – 7 cwt)
Saloon	Delivery van, 500 – 1000 kg
Estate	($\frac{1}{2}$ – 1 ton)
	Goods van, 1000 – 2000 kg
	(1 – 2 ton)
	Pantechnicon – high sided van
	Pick-up truck, 250 – 750 kg
	(5 – 15 cwt)
	Bus
	Rigid lorry, 1000 – 10 000 kg
	(1 – 10 ton)
	Coach
	Articulated lorry, over 10 000 kg
	(over 10 ton)

Pantechnicons and articulated lorries are generally referred to as heavy goods vehicles (HGV) and buses and coaches are known as public service vehicles (PSV).

Sports car

Sports body

A sports car body is shown in the illustration. The normal arrangement is to have a small low body, with only sufficient room for two people and their luggage. The top or hood is made from canvas or PVC and can be folded down. When the car is used in a cold or wet climate a glass-fibre hard-top is available as an accessory. This is more resistant to damage by the elements than a folding hood. The hard-top is often used in the winter and the hood in the summer.

Saloon body

This is the most popular type of private car body and a typical example is shown. Usually, the saloon seats between four and six people and it may have two or four doors. The boot is separate from the passenger compartment, and is at the rear in conventional cars and at the front in rear-wheel drive cars.

Saloon car

Van body

The van body is designed for carrying goods. The addition of seating for the passengers is optional, although one passenger seat is usually fitted next to the driver.

Estate car body

The estate car is also referred to as a traveller's car or a dual-purpose vehicle. It was originally used for people to travel around their estates or for commercial travellers. Estate uses were for shooting and fishing trips, carrying about six people and their equipment. The commercial traveller — probably the present major user — uses it with the rear seats folded down during the week to carry his wares and with the seats up at weekends for his family.

Van

Hatch-back

This is a combination of a saloon car and an estate car. The car's ability to carry goods and passengers whilst maintaining the looks of a saloon car has made it a very popular design.

Estate car

Rigid lorry

A typical rigid lorry is used for carrying goods on its flat, that is, its flat rear section. These are available to carry a variety of loads of up to about 10 tons.

Rigid lorry

Jacking points

Jacking points allow the driver to jack his car up easily by the roadside, for example, in the event of a puncture. They are specially shaped and strengthened areas designed to fit the jack, which is supplied in the car's tool kit. The point chosen is one where the car will be safely balanced and which is least likely to cause problems. However, it must be stressed that all the passengers must get out of the car and that all heavy luggage must be removed before attempting to jack the car up in this way.

There are two main types of jacking points: side jacking points and end jacking points. The side jacking point is in the sill. This type allows all the side of the car to be lifted up in one operation. This side type is used on small light cars. Heavy cars have four jacking points, one to lift each wheel off the ground. The illustration shows an end jacking point which will lift one wheel only. These are housed in the bumper/valance assembly.

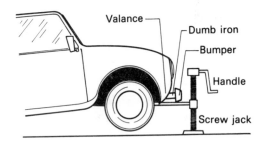

Jacking point (end)

Seats

Normally there are two bucket seats at the front of the car and a two- or three-seater bench seat at the rear. The part of the seat which is sat upon is called the *cushion* and the part which the back is rested against is called the *squab*. The rear seats are screwed or clipped to the body. The front bucket seats are adjustable to allow the driver to find a comfortable driving position. The seat-adjustment consists of a forwards and a backwards movement, with sometimes a raising and lowering cushion and a reclining

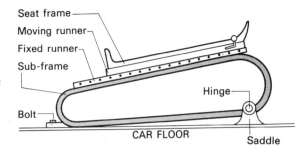

Seat-mountings

squab. A typical seat-mounting is shown in the diagram. This has a hinge at the front to allow the seat to be tilted forwards with a bar to lock it in place. A sliding runner is mounted on top of the sub-frame to give the seat a backwards and forwards movement. If the seat to the sub-frame mounting is inclined, this raises the cushion as the seat is moved forwards — a necessity for short drivers.

Seat belts

In various countries it is a legal requirement for cars to be fitted with seat belts. In the UK this applies to the front seats of cars manufactured since 1965.

The most popular seat-belt arrangement is the *lap and diagonal*. This has two straps running between three mounting points as shown in the diagram. One mounting point is on the floor in the centre of the car, another on the inside of the sill and the third is on the door pillar or the rear quarter panel. An alternative type of seat belt is the full harness seat belt. This has a full body harness mounted to four anchorage points.

The buckles of both types of belt must be quick-release. Generally, they can be operated by one hand, so that the occupants can leave the car quickly after an accident. This is particularly necessary if there is the risk of a fire starting or if the car is hit by another car, as in motorway pile-ups. The diagram shows a typical buckle or fastener.

The seat-belt mounting points or anchorages must be sufficiently strong to hold the passenger in place in the event of a collision. To ensure this, the mounting points are specially reinforced. To show that the mounting points are strong enough and comply with the various regulations (BS 48a), a plate is attached to either the body or chassis.

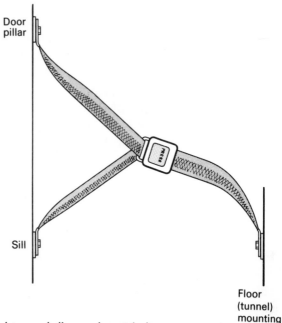

Lap and diagonal seat belt

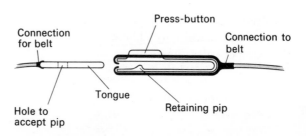

Seat-belt buckle

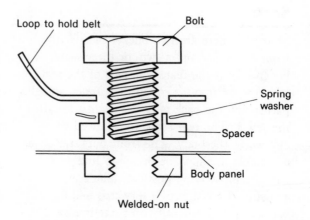

Seat-belt mounting

Corrosion-prevention

The natural state of iron and steel, is iron ore, or ferric oxide, i.e. rust. When the ore comes out of the ground it looks like pieces of rust. The steel which constitutes so much of the body shell of a motor car will rust and corrode very rapidly unless special preventive measures are taken. Since corrosion can drastically reduce the life of a car, manufacturers pay great attention to bodywork protection. The method of corrosion-prevention depends on the actual surface being treated. The table gives some examples.

Types of prevention	Materials from which the coating is made	Examples of use
Painting	Cellulose or acrylic	Outside of car
Undersealing	Rubber or wax	Underside of car
Chromium-plating	Chromium or nickel	Bright trim
Rubber-coating	Rubber	Bumpers and buffers
Galvanising	Zinc	Floors and areas open to weather

Multiple-choice questions

1 *Lap and diagonal* and *full harness* are types of:
   (a) chassis
   (b) body
   (c) seat belt
   (d) seat

2 Components known as *ladder* and *backbone* are types of:
   (a) body
   (b) chassis
   (c) seat
   (d) paint

3 How many people can normally be seated in a sports car:
   (a) 1
   (b) 6
   (c) 4
   (d) 2

4 Rubber body/chassis mountings are used to prevent:
   (a) corrosion
   (b) vibrations
   (c) overloading
   (d) noise

5 Two types of corrosion prevention are:
   (a) painting and undercoating
   (b) rubber coating and silver plating
   (c) painting and undersealing
   (d) galvanising and overcoating

6 A vehicle which has a front mounted engine driving the rear wheels is called:
   (a) conventional
   (b) normal
   (c) usual
   (d) chassis type

7 BS 48a refers to:
   (a) seat mountings
   (b) seat belt mountings
   (c) chassis mountings
   (d) chassis types

8 The noisiest vehicle layout is:
   (a) FWD
   (b) RWD
   (c) conventional
   (d) commercial

9 The two vehicle layouts which have flat floors are:
   (a) conventional and RWD
   (b) conventional and FWD
   (c) FWD and RWD
   (d) commercial and conventional

10 L and I are both types of:
   (a) chassis section
   (b) seat belt
   (c) body
   (d) commercial vehicle

2 The engine

The engine takes in fuel and air and burns it to create rotary motion or power. The amount of power developed depends on the size of the engine used. In a vehicle with a conventional layout the power transmitted through the clutch, the gearbox, the propeller-shaft and the rear axle must be sufficient to overcome the rolling friction of the wheels and the tyres, to drive the car against air resistance and to carry the vehicle, its load and its passengers up any gradient.

There are many different types of engines on the road today, the commonest being petrol and diesel engines, depending on which type of fuel they use. Petrol engines are also known as spark ignition (SI) engines because a spark plug is used, whereas diesel engines are referred to as compression ignition (CI) engines. Engines are also classified by the

Typical car engine

Typical lorry engine

number of strokes taken to complete a working cycle, i.e. how many times the piston has to go up and down to burn one charge of fuel and air. There are two-stroke engines and four-stroke engines. Summarising, then, we have two-stroke petrol engines and four-stroke petrol engines, and two-stroke diesel engines and four-stroke diesel engines.

The cylinder block forms the main part of the engine and carries the other components. The cylinder head controls the intake of the fuel and air through its valve mechanism. The connecting rod and crankshaft convert the reciprocating motion, i.e. the up and down movements of the piston, into rotary motion, which can be used to drive the car. The sump holds the necessary lubricating oil.

Each of the engine types are described fully in the following pages, and we will be able to see how the mixture is burnt differently in each case. However, all these engines are known as internal combustion engines. The combustion, or burning, of the mixture takes place inside the engine, above the piston.

The mixture of fuel and air is explosive. When its temperature reaches a certain level or if a spark is applied it will burn rapidly and violently. In the engine this rapid burning

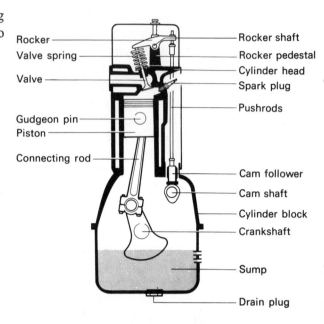

Main engine components

above the piston is controlled, so that the increase in pressure of the gas mixture forces the piston down the cylinder bore in the engine block. The downward force on the piston pushes on the connecting rod, which thereby rotates the crankshaft, so giving the necessary power or turning force to move the car.

Four-stroke petrol engine

The four-stroke petrol engine works on a system of four strokes to a complete cycle. This cycle is often called the *Otto cycle*. A stroke is the movement of the piston from the top to the bottom of the bore, and vice versa. One stroke corresponds to half a turn of the crankshaft, so a complete crankshaft revolution takes two strokes. Hence a complete cycle of four strokes takes two revolutions of the

crankshaft. When the piston is at the top of its stroke it is said to be at top dead-centre (TDC): when at the bottom of the stroke it is called bottom dead-centre (BDC). The four-stroke petrol engine is illustrated, viewed from the front in simple diagram form. Where appropriate, students are strongly advised to use this type of diagram to illustrate their examination questions.

The inlet and exhaust ports in the cylinder head connect the carburetter and exhaust system to the inside of the engine. When the piston is at TDC the space above it to the cylinder head is known as the combustion chamber. The valves close to seal the combustion chamber from the inlet and exhaust ports. When the valves are open the relevant gases can flow. The operation of the valves is controlled by the camshaft and rocker mechanism (this is described later in this chapter). We can now look at the details of each stroke in turn.

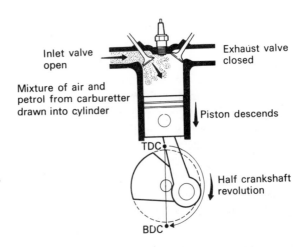

a *Induction stroke*

Induction stroke

The piston travels down the bore from TDC to BDC. This creates a partial vacuum above it which is filled by petrol and air being drawn in through the open inlet valve from the carburetter. This is like drawing liquid into a syringe. During this stroke the exhaust valve is closed.

Compression stroke

When the piston reaches BDC it starts to return up the bore. At BDC the inlet valve closes (the exhaust is already closed), so that, as the piston rises, the mixture of petrol and air above it (which was drawn in on the induction stroke) is compressed into the combustion chamber in the space left above the piston when it reaches TDC. This increases the pressure of the mixture to about 1250 kPa (180 psi). Depending on the compression ratio, the temperature of the mixture also increases.

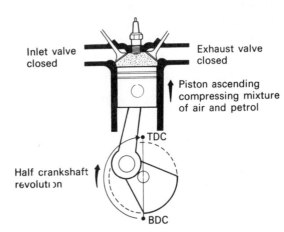

b *Compression stroke*

Power stroke

As the piston reaches TDC on the compression stroke the spark occurs at the spark plug. The ignition system is designed to produce a spark of about 10 kilovolts (kV) at exactly the right time. This spark ignites the compressed mixture of petrol and air so that as

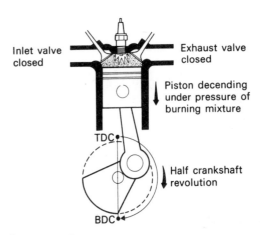

c *Power stroke*

the piston passes over TDC to start its downward stroke the temperature of the mixture reaches 2000°C. This increase in temperature causes an increase in pressure. The high pressure above the piston (about 5000 kPa/750 psi) forces the piston down the cylinder bore. The piston transmits its force through the gudgeon pin to the connecting rod, so turning the crankshaft, which turns the flywheel to drive the car through the transmission and road wheels. Both valves are tightly closed throughout this stroke.

Exhaust stroke

The exhaust valve opens and the piston reaches BDC on the power stroke, so that when the piston starts to ascend on the last stroke of the cycle the piston forces the hot (800°C) burnt gases out of the exhaust valve into the exhaust systems. At the end of the exhaust stroke the inlet valve opens and the cycle is repeated. This type of engine is used in the majority of passenger cars and light vans.

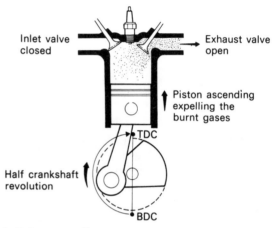

d *Exhaust stroke*

Two-stroke petrol engine

The two-stroke petrol engine is used mainly in small motor cycles, although some cars have used it. It operates on one up-stroke and one down-stroke of the piston, a method of combustion called the *Clerk cycle*. The two-stroke engine has no valves but it has three ports: the inlet port, the transfer port and the exhaust port. The flow of gas through these ports is controlled by the position of the piston. When the piston is at TDC the transfer and the exhaust ports are closed. When it is at BDC the piston skirt closes the inlet port.

The piston travels up the bore (see diagram). As it reaches TDC it closes the transfer and exhaust ports, at the same time compressing the charge of gas above it into the combustion chamber. At about TDC the spark plug ignites the mixture of petrol and air. The burning of this mixture increases the temperature and the pressure of the gas so that it pushes the piston down the bore. The downward force of the piston is passed through the gudgeon pin, so that the vehicle can be driven through its transmission system. On motor cycles this is usually a series of chains.

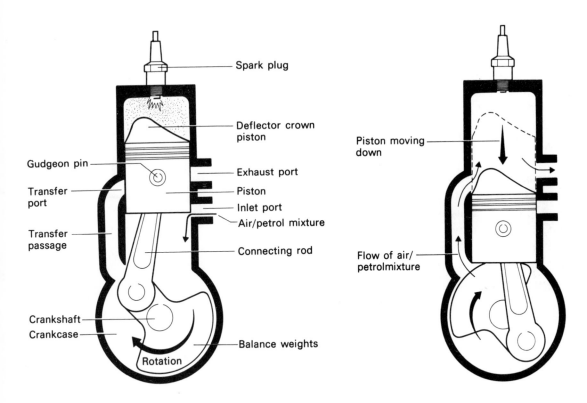

a *Two-stroke petrol engine: piston approaching TDC*

b *Two-stroke petrol engine: piston approaching BDC*

Whilst the piston is ascending its skirt uncovers the inlet port. The upward motion of the piston causes a vacuum in the crankcase which is filled by a petrol and air mixture from the carburetter entering through the now-open inlet port.

When the piston is travelling downwards (being forced down by the burning mixture) the exhaust port is first uncovered by the piston crown. This allows the spent gas to escape into the exhaust system. The skirt of the piston covers the inlet port at the same time as the piston crown uncovers the transfer port at the top of the cylinder. The underside of the piston therefore acts as a pump plunger, forcing the fresh charge in the crankcase up and through the transfer port into the cylinder

so that another cycle is started. The complete cycle takes two strokes of the piston (this being the same as one crankshaft revolution).

The two-stroke petrol engine is much lighter and simpler than the four-stroke petrol engine as it has fewer moving parts. It has no valves or valve-operating mechanism. This usually allows much higher running speeds than are possible with valved engines. Having one firing stroke per revolution should make the two-stroke engine twice as powerful as the equivalent-sized four-stroke. This is not the case, as the gas-compression and clearing away of the exhaust gases is not as efficient. However, its lightness and ability to run at high speeds makes it an ideal engine for motor cycles.

Four stroke diesel engines

The four-stroke diesel engine works in very much the same way as the four-stroke petrol engine. The main operational differences are that the petrol engine draws in a mixture of petrol and air from the carburetter, while the diesel engine draws in air only. Ignition of the petrol and air is by a spark plug, whereas in the diesel engine ignition occurs when the diesel fluid is injected into the hot compressed air above the piston. This is called *compression ignition* (CI), an alternative name for the diesel engine. The principle of operation was discovered by Dr Rudolf Diesel, after whom it was named.

The diesel engine differs from the petrol engine in that it does not have spark plugs to ignite the explosive mixture of air and fuel. The fuel used in the diesel engine is diesel oil, not petrol. Petrol and diesel oil are similar liquids to look at but they are easily identified by their different smells. The student is advised to make this distinction in smells by trying both so that he will not mistake the two liquids — an accident can cost much money and time if the wrong fuel is placed in a vehicle. The wrong fuel can severely damage the engine.

Unlike the petrol engine, the diesel engine does not draw in air and fuel together through a carburetter. The air, only, is drawn in through an air cleaner. A diesel engine does not have a carburetter. The air is compressed to a very high pressure which causes its temperature to increase. The diesel oil is then injected through a special device, called an injector, into the hot air. The high temperature of the air causes the diesel oil to ignite. The ensuing explosion then provides the power to send the piston down the cylinder bore turning the crankshaft via the connecting-rod.

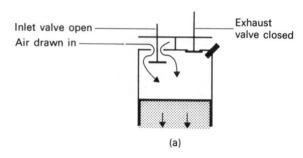

a *Diesel engine cycle: induction*

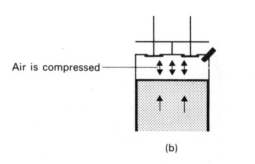

b *Diesel engine cycle: compression*

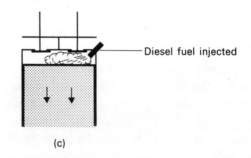

c *Diesel engine cycle: power*

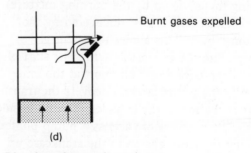

d *Diesel engine cycle: exhaust*

The four strokes of the diesel cycle, which takes two revolutions of the crankshaft to complete, have the same names as the corresponding petrol engine strokes.

Induction stroke
The inlet valve is open and the exhaust valve is closed. The piston travels down the cylinder bore causing a partial vacuum above it. This partial vacuum is filled by the entry of air from the air cleaner through the inlet manifold and the inlet valve. This is like drawing water into a garden syringe.

Compression stroke
As the piston rises from BDC to TDC both the inlet and the exhaust valves are closed. The upwards movement of the piston therefore compresses the air above it into the combustion chamber. The increase in pressure is very high in the diesel cycle. This is so that the air reaches the high temperature (about 450°C) needed to ignite the diesel fuel. The temperature of the air on this stroke can reach 600°C.

Power stroke
About 25 degrees before top dead-centre (TDC) the injector injects diesel fuel into the hot compressed air. The diesel fuel is atomised (broken into very small droplets) at a very high pressure (2500 psi (15 000 kPa)). This high pressure forces the atomised fuel into the cylinder so that it penetrates the compressed hot air. Diesel fuel spontaneously ignites at about 450°C so that the hot air sets the diesel fuel alight. As the piston reaches TDC the combustion process is well under way, so that the pressure of the burning gas forces the piston down the bore. As with the other types of engines, the gudgeon pin and connecting rod pass the power to the crankshaft, the rotating motion of which is used to drive the vehicle.

Exhaust stroke
Having completed its power stroke, the piston starts to ascend again. As it does so, it forces the burnt gases out of the now-open exhaust valve. The inlet valve is closed during this stroke.

Two-stroke diesel engines

As the diesel engine requires a high compression pressure, a supercharger or pump is used to force compressed air into the cylinder rather than crankcase pressure, as is used on the two-stroke petrol engine. It is also common practice to use a cam-operated exhaust valve to improve the engine's efficiency. Air is drawn into the blower and then forced under pressure into the annular port. When the piston is at BDC the air is allowed to pass through the ports into the cylinder. At this point the exhaust valve is open, allowing the gases to escape.

As the piston rises with its new charge above it the air is compressed, and the exhaust valve closed. As the pistons reaches TDC the injector injects fuel into the combustion chamber which burns and forces the piston down. The piston skirt cuts off the airflow from the ports. The piston uncovers the port through which compressed air at about 100 kPa (15 psi) enters the cylinder. This clean air also helps to eject the spent exhaust gases. The cycle then repeats itself: the piston rises, closing the exhaust valve and the air entry port for another compression and firing sequence.

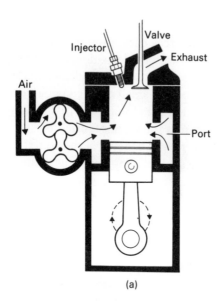

Two-stroke diesel engine. (a) Piston approaching BDC; (b) piston approaching TDC

The diesel engine is more efficient in four- and two-stroke forms than the equivalent-size petrol engine, i.e. per pound or kg of fuel it does more useful work. While this higher efficiency and lower cost has led to its widespread use in heavy goods vehicles, the diesel engine tends to be noisier and to produce smelly conditions compared with the petrol engine. It has therefore not yet achieved much popularity in the passenger car field.

Flywheel inertia

As there are two or four strokes to complete a cycle but only one firing stroke it is necessary to provide some means of turning the crankshaft and piston between the power strokes. The flywheel stores up energy in the form of inertia that keeps the engine turning between firing strokes.

Inertia is the tendency for an object, in this case the flywheel, once it is moving to keep moving, (in this case turning) until stopped by an equal force. So the flywheel must be sufficiently heavy to keep the engine turning. The greater the mass, or weight, of the flywheel the greater the inertia. Mass is given in kilogrammes (kg) or pounds (lb). More cylinders used in an engine allows the power strokes to be spaced out, so a smaller flywheel can be used. Engines with fewer cylinders need bigger flywheels.

Engine construction

As already mentioned, the engine consists of a few large components and many small ones. Most engines have more than one cylinder, so we must bear this in mind. We must also remember that each manufacturer produces several different engines, so there are many variations of the basic design. We are going to look at typical engine construction of the basic type by discussing the main components of both petrol and diesel engines.

Cylinder block

This is the main component around which the engine is built. The block is made from cast iron or, on certain cars, aluminium alloy. The cylinder block has the engine mounting attached to its outside for mounting to the vehicle's body or chassis. Bored vertically into the block are the cylinder bores. Engines are named according to the number of cylinders bored into the block, i.e. four- and six-cylinder engines. Engines have been made with sixteen cylinders, but those with more than eight are uncommon. The cylinder block must be rigid to hold the bores relative to each other and to hold the crankshaft in place. The crankshaft runs at right-angles to the cylinder bores, being retained in what are called main bearings. The block forms one semi-circular half of the bearing and a semi-circular cap forms the other half.

Shell bearings are used to keep the hardened steel crankshaft away from the cast iron cylinder block. This allows components to be manufactured to fine tolerances and reduces wear to a minimum. These shells have a steel outer casing which is pinched or clamped into the bearing of the cylinder block. The two half bearings are held together by high-tensile steel bolts and a soft metal lining in which the crankshaft runs. The soft metal is usually a combination of lead and tin, although copper and bronze are used in certain engines, mainly diesel engines.

A normal four-cylinder engine has either three main bearings, one at each end and one in the middle, or an arrangement of five, i.e. one between each cylinder. A six-cylinder engine has four, but where greater strength is needed these figures are increased to five and seven, respectively.

Mini Metro power unit

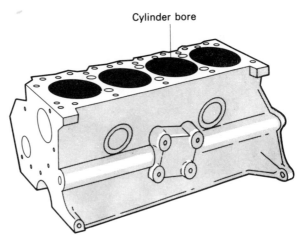

Cylinder bore

Cylinder block

As well as having the cylinder bores, main
bearings and engine mountings the cylinder
block has holes and tappings for such
components as the cylinder head, the water
pump, the sump, the generator, the valve
mechanism and the distributor.

Piston

The piston runs in the cylinder bore, going up
and down on stroke. Its purpose is to keep the
gases above and below it tightly sealed in their
place and to transmit the pressure of the
burning gases on the power stroke to the
gudgeon pin. Pistons are made from
aluminium alloy, which is light, strong and a
good conductor of heat. They look quite
simple but are extremely complicated. They
run at speeds of up to 13 m/s (2500 feet per
minute) with a temperature range being as
high as 2000°C at the crown and as low as
freezing point where the gudgeon pin fits. The
skirt is the lower half of the piston, being the
same shape as the garment it is named after.
Piston crowns come in different shapes: flat
top, dished and domed. These give different
combustion-chamber shapes. The skirt holds
the piston crown level by stopping the piston
from turning vertically in the bore of the
cylinder.

Piston: two rings are in place, two are missing

The aluminium of the piston expands faster
than the cast iron of the cylinder block. This
means that either the piston has to be made
smaller than the cylinder bore or that a split
has to be put in the piston skirt to take up the
expansion. Solid pistons, when hot, fit the
bore exactly (i.e. a running fit) but when these
pistons are cold they are too slack. The
movement of the piston in the bore is a
slapping side-to-side motion, called piston slap.
This can be heard clearly inside the car. Split
skirt pistons are the same size all the time.
The expansion of the piston simply closes the
split in the skirt.

Piston rings

As it is not possible to make the piston a running fit in the cylinder bore and a perfect gas-tight seal, piston rings are fitted. These rings are made from fine-grain cast iron. In some cases chromium is used to give extra life and reduced friction. Most pistons have three piston rings. The top two rings are to keep the gases in the cylinder and are called *compression rings*. The lower one prevents the oil splashed onto the cylinder bore from entering the combustion chamber, and is called an *oil ring*. On some pistons an extra ring is fitted at the bottom of the skirt. This is to reduce oil consumption, particularly on large diesel engines. The diagram shows cross-sections of the popular designs of piston rings. The oil drain hole in the piston is to allow the oil scraped from the bore to return to the sump from the inside of the piston.

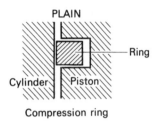
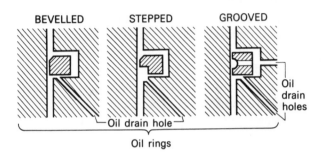

Types of piston rings

Gudgeon pin

The gudgeon pin is a hardened steel pin connecting the piston to the connecting rod. It fits into bosses or strengthened areas in the piston side and through the little end of the connecting rod. The gudgeon pin is free to rotate in either the little end of the connecting rod or the gudgeon pin bosses — sometimes in both. However, the gudgeon pin must be prevented from moving lengthways, as its hard surface can score a groove in the cylinder bore if it is allowed to rub. To prevent this movement, circlips are generally fitted in the gudgeon pin bosses. These are small spring rings which locate in grooves in the gudgeon pin bosses and project to stop the gudgeon pin floating out.

Connecting-rod

The connecting-rod little end is connected to the gudgeon pin. A bush made from a soft metal, such as bronze, is used for this joint. The lower end of the connecting-rod fits the

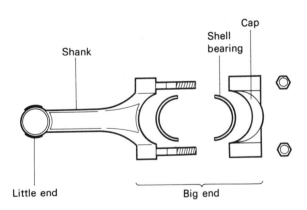

Connecting-rod. The shell bearings, cap and nut are shown in exploded form

crankshaft journal. This is called the *big end*. For this big-end bearing, steel-backed lead or tin shell bearings are used. These are the same as those used for the main bearings. The split of the big end is sometimes at an angle, so that it is small enough to be withdrawn through the cylinder bore. The connecting-rod is made from forged alloy steel.

Crankshaft

The crankshaft, in conjunction with the connecting-rod, converts the reciprocating motion of the piston to the rotary motion needed to drive the vehicle. It is usually made from carbon steel which is alloyed with a small proportion of nickel. The main bearing journals fit into the cylinder block and the big end journals align with the connecting rods. At the rear end of the crankshaft is attached the flywheel, and at the front end are the driving wheels for the timing gears, fan, cooling water and generator.

The throw of the crankshaft, i.e. the distance between the main journal and the big end centres, controls the length of the stroke. The stroke is double the throw, and the stroke-length is the distance that the piston travels from TDC to BDC and vice versa.

Flywheel

The flywheel fits onto the rear of the crankshaft. As well as keeping the engine rotating between power strokes (see flywheel inertia, page 24) it also carries the clutch, which transmits the drive to the gearbox, and has the starter ring gear around its circumference. The flywheel is made from carbon steel.

Sump

The sump is fitted at the bottom of the engine to collect and retain the lubricating oil. It is made of either steel pressings or cast aluminium.

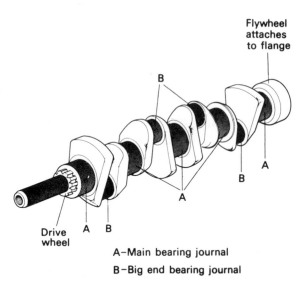

A – Main bearing journal

B – Big end bearing journal

Crankshaft for a four-cylinder engine

Flywheel

Cylinder head

The cylinder head fits, as its name implies, on top of the cylinder block. The underside forms the combustion chamber with the top of the piston. Generally the cylinder head is shaped so that the combustion chamber is actually in the cylinder head, the piston crown forming only one wall of the chamber. The cylinder head carries the valves, valve springs and the rockers on the rocker shaft, this part of the valve gear being worked by the pushrods.

Cylinder head. Two valves and springs are removed

Sometimes the camshaft is fitted directly into the cylinder head and operates on the valves without rockers. This is called an *overhead camshaft arrangement*. Like the cylinder block, the head is made from either cast iron or aluminium alloy. The cylinder head is attached to the block with high-tensile steel studs. The joint between the block and the head must be gas-tight so that none of the burning mixture can escape. This is achieved by using a cylinder head gasket. This is a sandwich gasket, i.e. a sheet of asbestos between two sheets of copper, both these materials being able to withstand the high temperature and pressures within the engine.

Valves

The flow of both the fresh incoming gases and the burnt outgoing gases are controlled by valves. These are made from expensive high-carbon steel alloys, using nickel and chromium which give hardness and resistance to wear. The exhaust valve, in particular, runs at several hundred degrees centigrade. The stem of the valve runs in a guide, which is pressed into the cylinder head and can easily be replaced when worn. The valve is held closed against its seat with a spring. The opening of the valve involves overcoming the forces of the spring and this is achieved by the camshaft and the valve mechanism. The actual seating surface of the valve to the head is a narrow

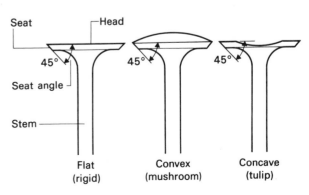

The three types of valves most commonly used

annular ring about 1/50th inch (0.5 mm) wide. This seat is cut at an angle of 45 degrees to the horizontal so that the valve is a taper fit into it, and hence a very tight seal is achieved.

Camshaft

The camshaft can be fitted into the cylinder block or the cylinder head. The former position, with rocker-operated valves in the cylinder head, is called an *overhead valve* (OHV) layout. The latter position, with the camshaft above the valves, is called an *overhead cam* (OHC) layout. The camshaft is driven by a chain connected to the front of the crankshaft. The camshaft has a separate cam for each valve, as each valve only opens once to each two revolutions of the crankshaft. It is sometimes more convenient to run the camshaft at half engine speed, and this is done through a 2:1 gearing, as shown in the diagram. The driving crankshaft gear wheel has half the number of teeth of the camshaft gear wheel. The formula for finding a gear ratio is:

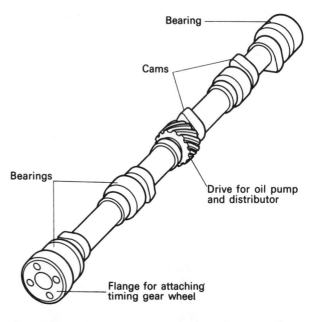

Camshaft

$$\text{Gear ratio} = \frac{\text{Number of teeth on driven wheel (camshaft)}}{\text{Number of teeth on driving wheel (crankshaft)}}$$

e.g. $\dfrac{50}{25} = \dfrac{2}{1}$

which is written 2:1 (: means 'to').

The timing gear ratio is always 2:1, even though different numbers of teeth are used. The camshaft always rotates at half the speed of the crankshaft.

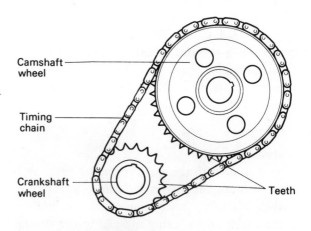

Camshaft timing gear ratio

The camshaft must open the valves at the correct time relative to the piston on the different strokes of the cycle. The chain drive ensures that the camshaft is timed to the engine in this way. Where more than one cylinder is used these are timed together by the position of the cams on the camshaft.

When we were discussing the various engine

cycles (page 19) we implied that the valves opened and closed instantaneously at TDC and BDC. As valves can neither open nor close straight away and as more power can be obtained by moving the opening and closing time, we have a slightly different valve timing. To get more gas into the cylinder the inlet valve starts to open about 10 degrees before top dead-centre (BTDC) and stays open until 40 degrees after bottom dead-centre (ABDC). The early opening is called *valve lead*. The exhaust valve opens at about 40 degrees

BBDC and closes 10 degrees ATDC so that the cylinder is thoroughly cleared of exhaust gases. The delay in closing is called *valve lag*. As the inlet stroke follows the exhaust stroke there is a period where both valves are open, i.e. 10 degrees BTDC to 10 degrees ATDC in our example. This is called *valve overlap*.

Valve mechanism

The two most commonly used mechanisms for opening and closing the valves are the overhead valve layout (OHV) and the overhead cam layout (OHC) as shown in the illustrations. The overhead cam layout has fewer moving parts than the overhead valve layout. This allows the engine equipped with the overhead camshaft to run at speeds higher than that of overhead valve engine. The overhead cam engine is currently used in many small modern family saloons as well as sportscars. However, the change to overhead cam has complicated engine overhaul procedures. The camshaft drive chain must be disconnected every time the cylinder head is

Rocker shaft

Rocker arm

Adjusting screw

Lock-nut

Spring

Pedestal

Valve

Port

Pushrod

Cam-follower

Cam

Overhead valve layout

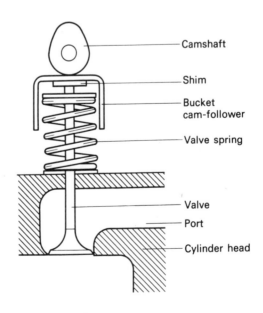

Camshaft

Shim

Bucket cam-follower

Valve spring

Valve

Port

Cylinder head

Overhead cam layout

removed. This means that the valve timing must be reset and the chain or drive belts readjusted.

Valve clearance

If the engine is to run correctly the valves must close tightly on their seats to produce a gas-tight seal and thus prevent the gases escaping from the combustion chamber. If the valves do not close fully the engine will not develop full power. Also the valve heads will be liable to be burnt by the passing hot gases, and there is the likelihood of the piston crown touching an open valve, which can seriously damage the engine.

So that the valves can close fully some clearance is needed in the operating mechanism. This means that the operating mechanism must be able to move sufficiently far enough away from the valve to allow the valves to be fully closed against its seat by the valve spring. However, if the clearance is set too great this will cause a light metallic tapping noise. This is usually referred to as *tappet rattle*.

The adjustment of the valve clearances on OHC engines is a complicated procedure involving the replacement of shims. This will be covered later in your course. However, the adjustment of valve clearances on OHV engines is a simple operation, providing that the correct procedure is followed.

To adjust the valve clearances it is essential that the valve to be set is fully closed and that the camshaft is in the correct position. The valve clearances are usually set one at a time, and the workshop manual for the particular model must be consulted to check the order of setting and what the exact clearance is. However, a common way of finding which valve clearance to set on a four-cylinder engine is to use 'the rule of nine'. The valves are

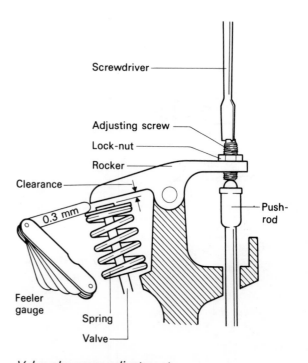

Valve-clearance adjustment

numbered 1 to 8, the valve at the free end or radiator end of the engine being number 1. See which valve is fully open, i.e. fully down. Subtract the number of that valve from 9, and the answer is the valve which is fully closed.

Having found which valve is closed and ready for setting, insert the correct size of feeler gauge. Slacken the lock-nut and turn the adjusting screw until the feeler gauge meets a light resistance. Finally, tighten up the lock-nut.

Number of valve open	Number of valve which can be set
1 $(9 - 1 = 8)$	8
2 $(9 - 2 = 7)$	7
3 $(9 - 3 = 6)$	6
4 $(9 - 4 = 5)$	5
5 $(9 - 5 = 4)$	4
6 $(9 - 6 = 3)$	3
7 $(9 - 7 = 2)$	2
8 $(9 - 8 = 1)$	1

Multi-cylinder arrangement

An engine with one cylinder has one power stroke followed by a series of non-working strokes so that a large flywheel is needed. The more powerful the engine is required to be the bigger and bulkier it becomes. It also vibrates as it fires, and is most uncomfortable for driver and passengers alike.

By increasing the number of cylinders the engine becomes more compact and smoother in running. The smoothness is achieved by arranging the cylinders so that their power strokes are in sequence, i.e. to have one cylinder fire at the front, then one at the opposite end, until all have fired and the sequence starts again. This sequence is called the *firing order*. For four-cylinder engines firing orders $1-3-4-2$ and $1-2-4-3$ are used, whilst six-cylinder engines have a wider choice, typical firing orders being $1-3-2-6-4-5$, $1-3-5-6-4-2$, $1-4-5-6-3-2$ and $1-4-2-6-3-5$.

The four-cylinder engine therefore has two power strokes for each crankshaft revolution, i.e. one every 180 degrees, whilst the six-cylinder engine has three power strokes per revolution, i.e. one every 120 degrees. V8 and V6 engines have more complicated arrangements, and sometimes the spacing is not exactly equal.

Differences between SI and CI engines

Petrol (SI) and diesel (CI) engines are very similar in contruction and operating cycle. The different fuel systems and the absence of spark plugs on CI engines are often the only outward sign on an engine which is not running. As we said earlier, the diesel is more noisy and has a different smell to the petrol engine. However, firms such as Austin-Morris, Peugeot, Volkswagen and Mercedes have introduced new diesel models which almost equal the petrol engines in these respects.

As higher temperatures and pressures are used on the diesel engine compression stroke and as a different ignition is used, the component parts of the diesel engine must be stronger and hence heavier than a petrol engine. The heavier parts and CI process also require a slower running speed. A normal petrol engine runs up to about 6000 rpm whilst a diesel which runs over 2000 rpm (say, 2200 rpm) is called a high-speed diesel.

Engine capacity
Engine capacity is the swept volume (see below) of all of the cylinders. This is defined by the formula

$$\frac{\pi\, d^2 L}{4} \times N = \text{engine capacity}$$

where d = cylinder diameter (bore),
L = length of stroke,
N = the number of cylinders.

Compression ratio
The compression ratio is the amount by which the gas is compressed into the combustion chamber. The formula for finding the compression ratio (CR) is:

$$CR = \frac{SV + CV}{CV}$$

SV means swept volume, i.e. the actual

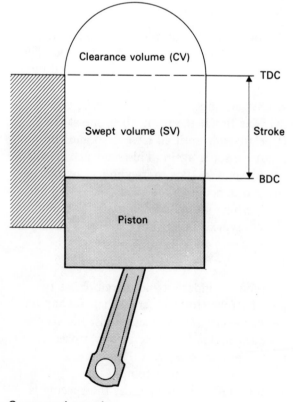

Compression ratio

volume of the cylinder in cubic centimetres (cc). The swept volume is calculated by the formula:

$$SV = \frac{\pi d^2 L}{4}$$

Where d = cylinder diameter (or bore) and L = length of stroke. CV is the clearance volume, i.e. the space above the piston when the piston is at TDC. The CV is calculated by

using a measuring cylinder calibrated in cubic centimetres.

The higher the compression ratio the higher the temperature and the pressure on the compression stroke. Typical compression ratios are:

Ordinary family cars (petrol)	7:1 to 9:1
Sports cars and motor cycles (petrol)	9:1 to 11:1
Racing cars and motor cycles (petrol)	11:1 to 13:1
Diesel engines	14:1 to 22:1

Multiple-choice questions

1 *Induction* and *power* are two strokes of the four stroke cycle, the other two are called:
   (a) exhaust and clearance
   (b) compression and exhaust
   (c) clearance and compression
   (d) sweeping and compressing

2 The flywheel stores:
   (a) inertia
   (b) oil
   (c) power
   (d) petrol

3 The formula for compression ratio is:

   (a) $\dfrac{sv + cv}{sv}$

   (b) $\dfrac{sv + sv}{cv}$

   (c) $\dfrac{sv + cv}{cv}$

   (d) $\dfrac{sv}{cv + sv}$

4 On the induction stroke the petrol engine draws in a mixture of petrol and air, the diesel engine draws in:
   (a) diesel and petrol and air
   (b) diesel and air
   (c) diesel only
   (d) air only

5 The camshaft turns at:
   (a) crankshaft speed
   (b) half crankshaft speed
   (c) quarter crankshaft speed
   (d) twice crankshaft speed

6 The temperature inside the combusition chamber on ignition is approximately:
   (a) 2000°C
   (b) 200°C
   (c) 1000°C
   (d) 100°C

7 The component which connects the piston to the connecting rod is the:
   (a) split pin
   (b) gudgeon pin
   (c) clevis pin
   (d) ankle pin

8 Two types of valve mechanism layout are:
  (a) under cam and under valve
  (b) overhead valve and lower head valve
  (c) overhead valve and overhead cam
  (d) side valve and bottom valve

9 The cylinder block is usually made from:
  (a) wrought iron
  (b) cast iron
  (c) mild steel
  (d) cast steel

10 A typical firing order for a four cylinder engine is:
  (a) 1432
  (b) 4123
  (c) 1234
  (d) 1342

3 The fuel system

The fuel system supplies the vehicle with the necessary amount of fuel for it to be able to do its work efficiently. The engine must receive the correct amount of fuel at the correct time, or else it will not run properly — if at all. A car uses fuel like a human uses food. The correct amount and type are needed to give health and vigour. A person who eats too much becomes fat and slow; one who does not eat enough will waste away. The same applies to an engine. Just as people choose different diets, so different engines use different fuels. The two main choices are petrol and diesel, though vehicles have been made to run off coal, wood, paraffin and even gunpowder. These fuels are called hydrocarbons, as they contain hydrogen and carbon. They are all burnt in air.

Petrol supply system

The layout of a typical petrol supply system is shown in the diagram. The main components are the petrol tank, the petrol pump and the carburetter. All these components are connected by a small pipe which is called a petrol pipe, or a fuel line.

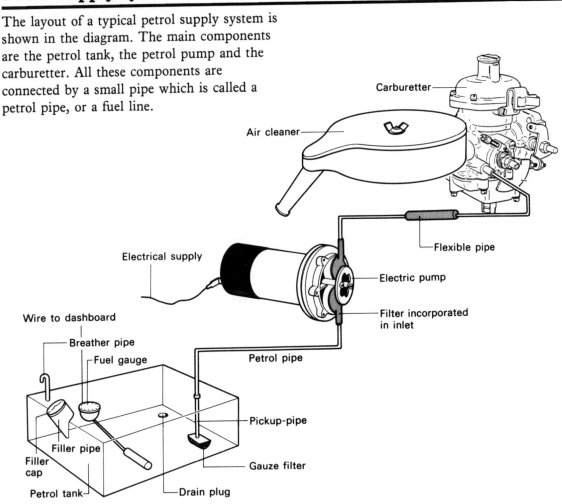

Layout of petrol supply system

Petrol tank

The petrol tank is made from low-carbon steel. This material is strong and tough, and it is not liable to fracture on impact during a collision or if hit by a flying stone. It will bend and crumple without spilling its contents over the car or on the road. Remember that *petrol is highly flammable*— it can be ignited by a single spark or flash. Remember also that petrol gives off fumes which are *explosive*.

The petrol tank is designed to give the car a reasonable cruising range based roughly on an average day's drive. This is about 300 miles, so if the car's fuel consumption is about 30 mpg, the tank capacity will be found by the formula:

$$\text{Capacity} = \frac{\text{Average day's drive}}{\text{Miles per gallon (mpg)}}$$

$$= \frac{300}{30} = 10 \text{ gallons}$$

Cars which are meant to be driven long distances each day and cars which have a high fuel consumption will have correspondingly larger tanks. Let us say the car is meant to travel 400 miles per day and has a consumption of 20 mpg:

$$\text{capacity of tank} = \frac{400}{20} = 20 \text{ gallons}$$

On the continent, the capacity of the petrol tank is calculated using SI units. In this system the fuel consumption of the car is given in litres per 100 km e.g 10 litres per 100 km, which means that the engine will consume a total of 10 litres in travelling a distance of 100 km. Therefore, assuming an average day's drive of 500 km and a fuel consumption of 10 litres per 100 km, the petrol tank capacity would be calculated as:

$$500 \times \frac{10}{100} = 50 \text{ litres.}$$

The petrol tank is fitted with a sensor unit to measure how much petrol is in the tank. This is connected to the petrol gauge on the dashboard, so that the driver can see at any time how much petrol is in the tank. This sensor device is referred to as a *tank unit*. The tank unit fits into the tank through a hole on the top or side. At the bottom of the tank is a drain plug. Petrol is drawn out of the tank through a pick-up pipe which fits into the top of the petrol tank and extends to within about 2 mm of the bottom. To prevent the pick-up pipe from drawing up dirt and scale it is fitted with a gauze filter around its bottom end. This filter if often called a primary filter. The tank also has a breather pipe which allows air to enter to fill up the space left by the outgoing petrol. By law the tank is mounted outside the passenger compartment of the car, well away from the passengers. This lessens the risk of injury to passengers by fire.

Petrol pump

Petrol pumps can be mechanically or electrically operated, and are therefore referred to as mechanical and electrical petrol pumps, respectively. The mechanical petrol pump is mounted on the engine, being driven by the camshaft. The electric pump is mounted on the chassis near the petrol tank. Electricity is delivered to it when the ignition is switched on.

Operation of petrol pump

The diagram shows schematically the inside of the petrol pump. Mechanical or electrical power, depending on the type of pump, pulls down the rod, and the rod pulls down the diaphragm against the pressure of the spring. The downwards movement of the diaphragm increases the size of the pumping chamber creating a partial vacuum above it, and this is filled by the petrol entering through the one-way valve on the inlet side. This is similar to the induction stroke of the engine itself. At the

end of the downward stroke the rod is freed
from the pull of the mechanical/electrical
force, so the pressure of the spring forces the
diaphragm upwards. The upwards movement
of the diaphragm forces the petrol out of the
one-way outlet valve to the carburetter. The
pressure of the petrol entering the carburetter
is between about 30 and 50 kpa (5–7 psi).

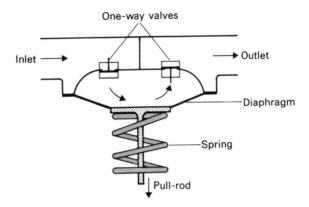

Layout of petrol pump

Petrol pipes

The pipes which carry the petrol along the
chassis are mainly made from steel, although
in some cases plastic pipes are used. However,
where flexibility is needed from the chassis to
the engine to accomodate the movements of
the engine, a steel-braid covered rubber pipe is
used.

Carburetter

The carburetter mixes petrol and air in the
correct proportions to be burnt inside the
engine.

The simple carburetter

The basic principles of carburation are
embodied in the simple carburetter. Petrol is
in the float chamber, which is connected to the
discharge jet through a tube containing a main
metering jet. When the engine is turned over
with the throttle valve open and the choke
butterfly open, air is drawn into the venturi.
The venturi is the name given to the section of
the air passage through the carburetter where
its diameter is decreased and the fuel discharge
nozzle is situated. The venturi is sometimes
called the choke tube. The narrowing of the
passage causes the air-speed to increase and the
pressure to decrease. The petrol therefore
flows and mixes with the air to be drawn into
the engine. The throttle controls the air and
petrol flow, and therefore the speed of the
engine. The choke controls the mixture
strength by limiting the flow of air alone. The
choke is for cold starting only.

Variable-choke carburetter

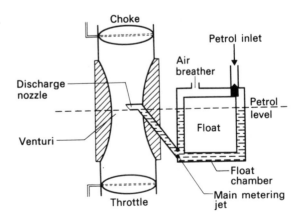

Simple carburetter

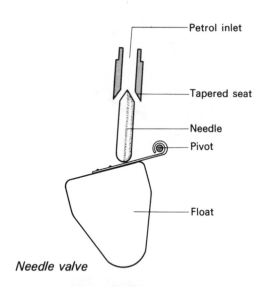

Needle valve

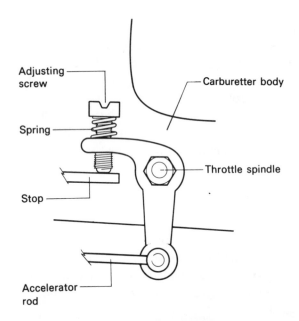

Adjusting idling speed. To speed up the engine, turn the screw clockwise

The flow of petrol into the float chamber is controlled by the needle valve. As the float chamber fills, the float rises. The float pushes the needle valve up against its seat and stops the flow of petrol.

The simple carburetter is only found on constant output engines, like those used on lawnmowers. This type of carburetter is not suitable for road vehicles as it has no provision for acceleration or cruising.

Air:petrol ratio

Different air to petrol ratios are needed for different conditions, examples are given in the table. The full range of ratios is achieved by most modern carburetters. Some adjustment is possible on most carburetters, so that the correct slow running speeds and mixture strengths can be achieved. The diagrams show these adjustments being carried out.

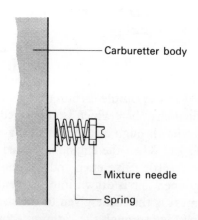

Adjusting mixture strength. To enrich the mixture, turn the mixture needle clockwise

Condition	Air:Fuel
Cold starting	9:1
Slow running	13:1
Accelerating	11:1
Cruising	17:1

Air cleaner

The air cleaner has three functions:

1 To clean the air as it enters the engine, thereby preventing the entry of dust and grit which might damage the inside of the engine.
2 To silence air movement, so making the engine less noisy.
3 To act as a flame trap, so preventing a serious fire should the engine backfire.

There are two types of air cleaner, the paper element type and the oil bath type. The paper element type is very simple. The paper filters out the dirt, and when it is dirty it can be thrown away and replaced with a new one. The oil-bath air cleaner uses about 1/4 pint (0.14 litre) of oil and a section of wire gauze. When the filter is dirty it can be washed out in paraffin and filled with clean oil.

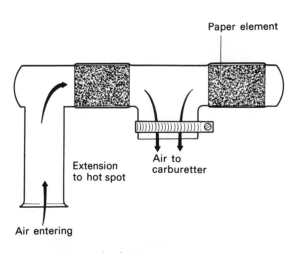

Paper element air cleaner

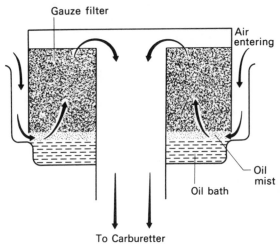

Oil bath air cleaner

Diesel supply system

The main difference between petrol systems and diesel fuel supply systems is that whereas petrol is mixed with air as it enters the engine, diesel is forced into the engine separately under pressure. The tank of a diesel lorry is very large, having a capacity of at least 230 l (50 gallons). This is because diesel lorries use a lot of fuel and cover large distances.

Injector pump

Fuel is pumped from the tank by a lift pump which operates and looks like a petrol pump. The lift pump delivers the petrol to the injector pump. There are two different types of injector pumps, the in-line type and the DPA type (distributor pump assembly). Both types of pump control the amount and the

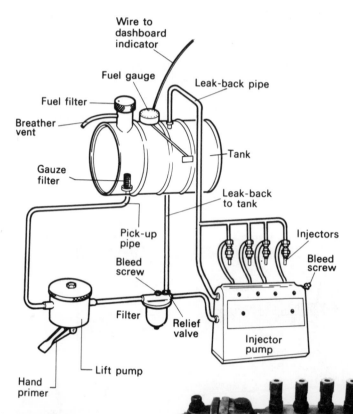

Diesel fuel system (not to scale)

timing of the fuel injected. The further the accelerator pedal is depressed the more fuel is injected. The pump sends the fuel to the injector at about 150 bar (15 000 kPa).

Jerk pump

The in-line diesel injector pump is made up from a series of jerk pumps, one for each cylinder. The pump camshaft is driven from the timing gears. When it rotates, the cam moves the plunger up the barrel. The upward stroke of the plunger pumps diesel fuel to the injector pump. The rack is controlled by the accelerator pedal. Moving the rack rotates the relative positions of the plunger and the barrel. These components are specially shaped to regulate, or control, the amount of fuel

In-line diesel injection pump

DPA rotary injection pump

delivered on each stroke of the plunger. This controls the power output of the engine.

Beware: diesel fuel is unclean, so barrier-creams must be used to reduce the risk of contracting dermatitis. A clean, synthetic diesel fuel is used when diesel components are being tested or repaired.

Injectors

The injector is fitted into the cylinder head. It projects into the combustion chamber so that it can inject diesel fuel into the hot air just before TDC on the compression stroke. The injector is designed so that the fuel is injected at a more or less constant pressure. The spray from the injector is in the form of a fine mist, often referred to as atomised. The inside of an injector is shown in the diagram. Injectors should be overhauled and adjusted at set service intervals.

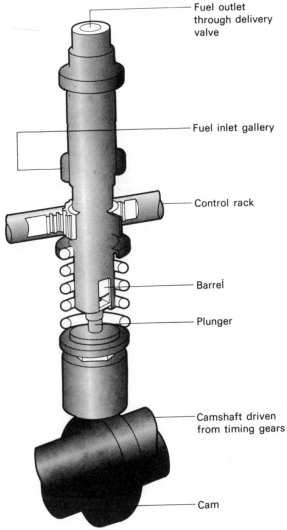

Jerk pump

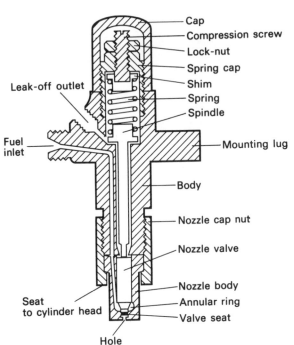

Diesel injector

Multiple-choice questions

1 The petrol tank must, by law, be fitted:
   (a) under the bonnet
   (b) inside the passenger compartment
   (c) inside the boot
   (d) outside the passenger compartment

2 As well as cleaning the air, the air cleaner:
   (a) acts as a silencer and flame trap
   (b) acts as a dryer and silencer
   (c) operates the choke mechanism
   (d) operates a flame wall and oiler

3 The component which pumps diesel fuel at high pressure to the injector is called:
   (a) injector pump
   (b) lift pump
   (c) air pump
   (d) compressor

4 The air:fuel ratio at cruising speed is:
   (a) 11:1
   (b) 20:1
   (c) 15:1
   (d) 17:1

5 The carburetter needle valve controls the:
   (a) amount of air
   (b) level of petrol
   (c) mixture strength
   (d) slow running speed

6 The function of the carburetter is to:
   (a) mix petrol and water
   (b) mix air and oil
   (c) mix petrol and air
   (d) charge the battery

7 *Plunger* and *barrel* are both components in the:
   (a) carburetter
   (b) alternator
   (c) injector pump
   (d) petrol pump

8 The purpose of the injector is to:
   (a) inject diesel fuel into the combustion chamber
   (b) inject air into the combustion chamber
   (c) give a richer mixture for acceleration
   (d) clean the air cleaner

9 There are two types of petrol pump, these are:
   (a) electrical and pneumatic
   (b) mechanical and electrical
   (c) solenoid and magnetic
   (d) hand and electrical

10 To accomodate movement between the engine and the chassis the fuel line is fitted with a:
   (a) connector
   (b) filler
   (c) steel pipe
   (d) flexible pipe

4 The ignition system

The purpose of the ignition system is to provide a spark in the combustion chamber which will ignite the mixture of petrol and air whilst it is under pressure. As the piston compresses the gases into the combustion chamber on the compression stroke the pressure of the gas above the piston is increased to about 1000 kPa (150 psi). The voltage needed for a spark to jump a spark gap at this high pressure is about 10 kV (10 000 V).

Typical ignition system

The layout of a typical ignition system is shown. This system is often referred to as the Kettering system, having been invented by Dr Kettering at the beginning of this century. The main components of the ignition system are battery, coil, spark plugs and distributor.

Battery
The battery is the source of electrical power for the ignition system, and it is found under the bonnet. The power enters the ignition circuit through the ignition switch which serves to make and break the ignition circuit. When the engine is not running the ignition switch must be switched off to disconnect the electrical supply and so prevent the coil from overheating. The ignition switch is also a thiefproofing device serving to prevent the car from being used unlawfully. The ignition switch is usually combined with the steering-lock, so that one key is used to unlock the steering and switch on the ignition. The steering/ignition lock is situated under the dashboard next to the steering column, where it is convenient for the driver.

Coil
The ignition coil is a kind of transformer. It changes the 12 V from the battery through the ignition switch into 10 kV at the spark plugs.

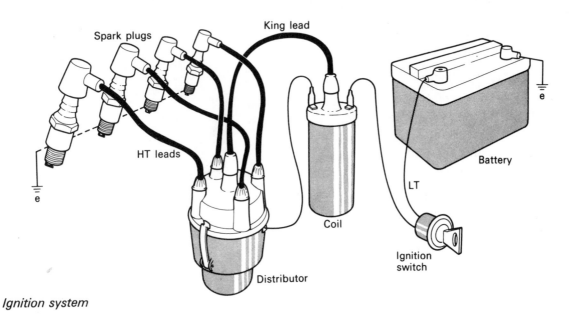

Ignition system

The section of the ignition circuit which carries the 12 V electrical items is called the primary circuit or the low tension (LT) circuit. The section of the circuit which carries the high 10 kV is called the secondary circuit, or high tension (HT) circuit. 10 kV means 10 kilovolts, i.e. 10 000 V.

The coil has three electrical terminals, one to the ignition switch, one to the distributor body and one to the distributor cap. The connections to the ignition switch and distributor are low tension. The other one, to the cap, is the high-tension connection.

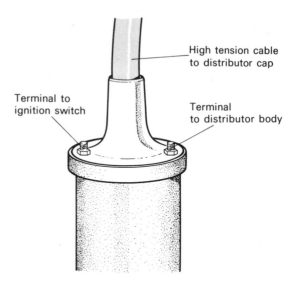

Ignition coil

Spark plugs

The metal end of the spark plug screws into the cylinder head so that the electrode protrudes into the combustion chamber. The screw thread with the washer and mating surfaces form a gas-tight seal, so preventing the loss of gases from the cylinder.

The diameter and the reach of the spark plug varies from engine to engine. The most common diameters of plug are 10 mm, 14 mm and 18 mm. The common reaches are $\frac{3}{8}$ inch, $\frac{1}{2}$ inch and $\frac{3}{4}$ inch. It is important that the correct diameter and reach of spark plug is fitted in any engine. The spark plug can be identified by the letters and numbers stamped on its body. When the spark plugs are replaced, at about 15 000-km (10 000-mile) intervals, they should be replaced with the same number of spark plug. The numbers can be checked in either the workshop manual or the plug-manufacturer's guide.

Servicing of the spark plug consists of cleaning them to remove any carbon deposits every 7500 km (5000 miles) and resetting their gaps. To clean the plugs effectively a plug-cleaning machine should be used. Before replacing them they should be gapped, i.e. the gap set to the manufacturer's figures and tested in the

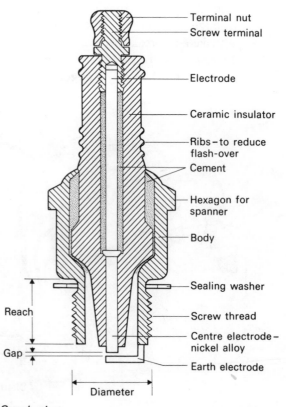

Spark plug

plug-cleaning machine. Every 15 000 km (10 000 miles) the plugs should be replaced with new ones with correctly adjusted gaps.

Distributor

The diagram shows a typical distributor. Inside it is divided into three parts: the lower part houses the mechanical components and the linkages, the middle part comprises the LT components and the upper part is the HT section. The HT components are mainly the cap and the rotor arm. HT electricity is delivered from the coil to the centre of the cap.

Electricity flows from the cap to the rotor arm through a brush arrangement. The rotor arm is connected to the distributor spindle so that it goes around at the same speed as the spindle. As the rotor arm rotates its free end aligns with segments in the distributor cap one at a time. The sequence is the firing order. As each segment is aligned the current is passed from the rotor arm to the segment. The segments each have a plug lead attached to carry the electricity on its way to the spark plug.

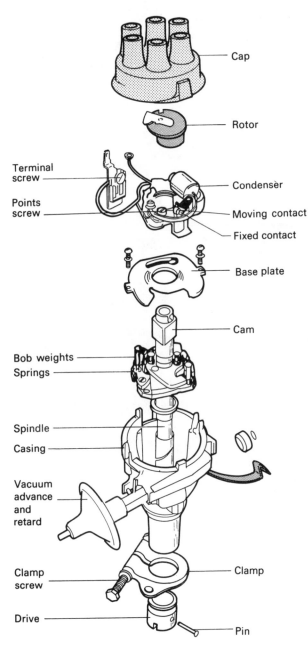

Distributor

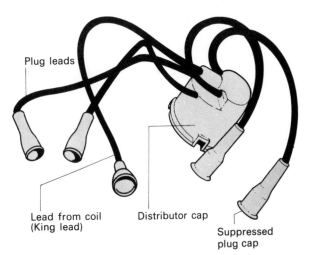

Distributor cap and plug leads

The low-tension part of the distributor comprises the contact breaker (cb) points and the capacitor. The cam ring which is formed on the outside of the distributor spindle rotates at the same speed as the spindle. As the cam goes round it opens and closes the cb points. It is this action which causes the current to flow in the HT circuit by inductions in the coil. The gap of the cb points, and their position in relation to the spindle, affect the ignition timing and general efficiency. The cb points should be checked for condition and size of gap every 7500 km (5000 miles). They should be replaced every 15 000 km (10 000 miles). The illustration shows how cb points are removed and replaced. The capacitor is fitted to give longer cb point-life by limiting arcing and to give a good quality spark by controlling the flow of electricity.

The drive for the distributor is picked up from the camshaft by an angular gear called a skew gear. This skew gear is on the lower end of the distributor spindle. The spindle passes through the mechanical and vacuum timing mechanisms which advance and retard the ignition timing with varying engine speed and load characteristics. The distributor rotates at the same speed as the camshaft, i.e. half the speed of the crankshaft.

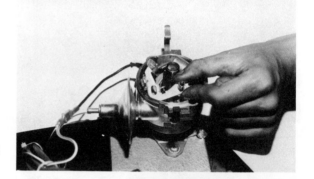

Changing contact breaker points.
(a) Removing moving contact; (b) removing fixed contact; (c) using screwdriver and feeler gauges to adjust points gap

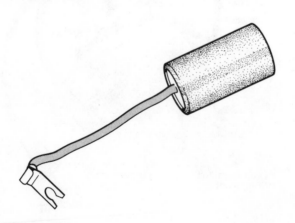

Capacitor

Ignition timing

The spark should occur just before Top Dead-Centre (TDC). Each manufacturer gives a specific figure for each of their vehicles. The static timing can be checked by using a small bulb on two pieces of wire. One of the free ends of the wire is attached to the coil to the distributor side terminal (i.e. LT) and the other free end is connected to earth. The HT lead or plug leads are disconnected so that the engine will not start when the ignition is switched on. The engine is turned over slowly by hand, observing the timing marks and the bulb. The bulb should light just as the marks align. Adjustment can be made by moving the distributor in its clamp to the engine.

A circuit diagram for a four-cylinder engine's ignition circuit is illustrated. This kind of diagram is often found in the workshop manual for the specific vehicle. The exact wiring can be seen, and this is necessary for fault-finding and for identifying the components.

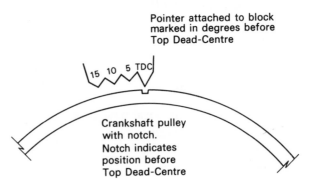

Timing marks

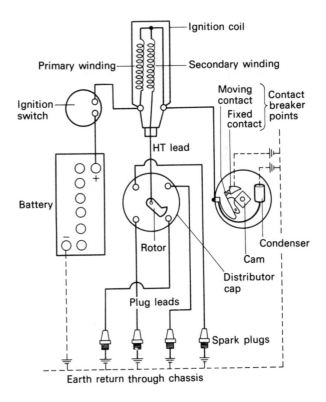

Diagram for a four-cylinder engine's ignition circuit

Multiple-choice questions

1   The system which provides a high voltage spark to the spark plugs is the:
(a) charging system
(b) ignition system
(c) lighting system
(d) starting system

2   The source of electrical power for the ignition system is the:
(a) battery
(b) coil
(c) distributor
(d) starter

3   The ignition coil gives an output of:
(a) 1kV
(b) 10kV
(c) 100kV
(d) 1000kV

4   Electrode, body and terminal are all found on the:
(a) distributor
(b) battery
(c) coil
(d) spark plug

5   The spark at the plugs occurs at:
(a) ATDC
(b) BTDC
(c) ABDC
(d) BBDC

6   The distributor is driven by the:
(a) camshaft
(b) fan belt
(c) crankshaft
(d) timing chain

7   The component which prevents arcing at the cb points is the:
(a) coil
(b) distributor
(c) capacitor
(d) king lead

8   The component in the ignition system which is designed to prevent theft is the:
(a) battery
(b) rotor arm
(c) ignition switch
(d) earth lead

9   Spark plugs should be cleaned every:
(a) 1000 km
(b) 5000 km
(c) 10 000 km
(d) 7500 km

10   The condition of the cb points should be checked every:
(a) 7500 km
(b) 10 000 km
(c) 1000 km
(d) 5000 km

5 The cooling system

The purpose of the cooling system is to keep the engine at a constant temperature whilst preventing overheating of any specific components. The average car petrol engine runs most efficiently at between 80° and 85°C. Diesel lorry engines run at about 5° cooler. There are two types of cooling systems: water cooling and air cooling.

Water cooling system

Water has a natural tendency to circulate when heated up in the cooling system—hot water rises. This is called thermo-syphoning. As the cooling water is heated up in the cylinder block it rises through the top hose into the radiator header tank. The water then falls through the radiator core into the bottom tank. As it falls it is cooled by the incoming air which passes through the radiator from the front of the car.

The weight of the water in the radiator forces it through the bottom hose back into the engine. The water can then continue thermo-syphoning provided that there is enough water in the system. The water level must be kept above the top of the top hose connection to ensure that a constant circulation is maintained.

Water pump
To circulate the water quickly a water pump is fitted. This forces the water to circulate around the engine in the same direction as the thermo-syphoning. The water pump is fitted onto the front of the engine. The bottom hose from the radiator is connected to the water pump and the water outlet from the pump is connected to the engine's water jacket. The pump is driven by the fan belt from the crankshaft pulley. The same belt turns the generator and the cooling fan.

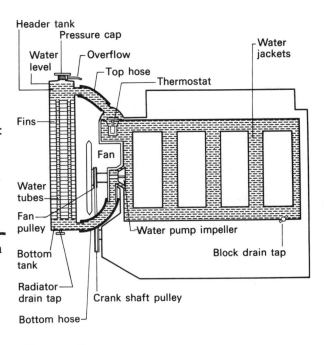

Water cooling system

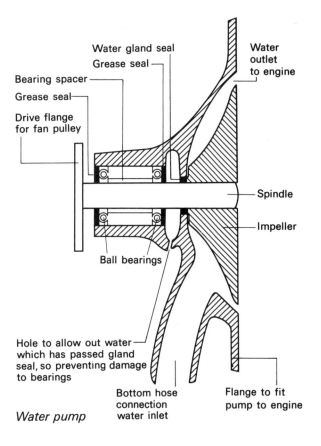

Water pump

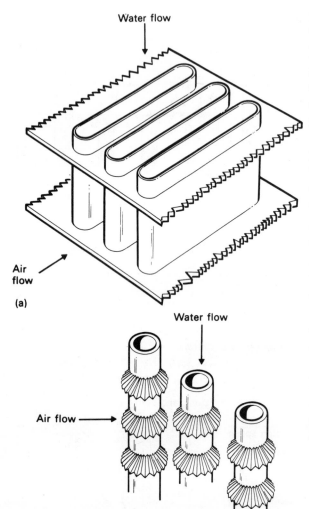

(a)

Fan

The fan is turned when the engine is running. It is mounted on the water pump spindle and is driven by the fan belt. Its movement draws air through the radiator. As the cool air flows over the radiator fins it cools the water in the radiator.

Radiator

The radiator is made up of the header tank, the bottom tank and the core between them. The diagram shows details of various types of core contruction. The flattened tube type of construction is used on most light vehicles; heavy goods vehicles tend to use the round tube variety; luxury cars use the very expensive honeycomb variety. The radiator has fins which increase the surface area of the cooling zone. This dissipates the heat more efficiently.

An alternative form of radiator is the *cross-flow* type. This is not as tall as the conventional type, as the tanks are at each end. The water flows from one side to the other, i.e. across the radiator. This type of radiator is used on sports cars where a very low bonnet is needed.

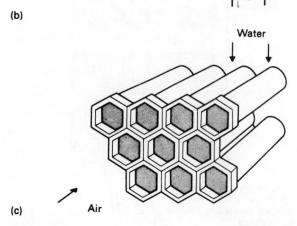

(b)

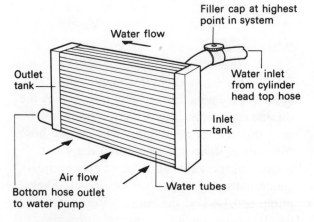

(c)

Radiator cores. (a) Flattened tube; (b) round tube; (c) honeycomb

Cross-flow radiator

Thermostat

The thermostat is a temperature-operated water valve. It is fitted between the top of the engine and the top hose. A connection, usually a separate casting called a thermostat housing, is used to locate it. When the thermostat is closed the water cannot flow; when it is open the water can flow. The thermostat allows a quick warm-up period by remaining closed until the engine has reached its required temperature and keeps the engine at a constant temperature by opening and closing as the engine becomes hot or cools down.

The thermostat shown in the diagram is a wax thermostat. The metal body or capsule (1) is filled with wax (2) which expands its volume very rapidly at certain temperatures. Normal opening temperature for a thermostat is around 80°C. When the wax in such a thermostat reaches the marked temperatures (this temperature is stamped on the thermostat flange (6)) the wax rapidly expands, forcing the thrust pin (3) out of the capsule against the pressure of the return spring. The thrust pin lifts the moving valve (4), so allowing the water to flow from the engine to the radiator via the top hose. When the wax cools, it contracts. The return spring closes the valve and returns the thrust pin into the capsule. The jiggle pin (5) is fitted to prevent a vacuum in the engine's water jacket by allowing tiny amounts of water to flow, even when the thermostat is closed.

Pressure cap

At normal atmospheric pressure, water in the radiator boils at 100°C. At high altitudes the boiling temperature is reduced. To prevent overheating and boiling over, a radiator pressure cap is fitted. The pressure of the spring ensures that the water is kept under pressure. The higher the pressure, the higher the boiling point of the water in the cooling

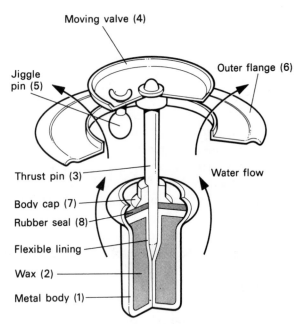

Wax thermostat (open). The valve is closed by an external spring (not shown)

system. Pressure caps of between 5 psi and 15 psi are used. To prevent the build-up of a vacuum a spring is fitted. This stops the radiator collapsing when it cools and the water pressure decreases.

The diagram show a cross-sectional view of a radiator pressure cap. The actual retaining cap (1) is secured to the radiator neck (2) with two curved sections. The radiator cap is fitted to the radiator in a similar way to a lid on a jam jar. The pressure seal (3) is held in place against the top of the radiator (6) by the pressure spring (4). Only when the water pressure exceeds the pre-set figure (which is stamped on the top of the cap) is the seal lifted against the spring pressure. The cooling water is then ejected through the overflow pipe (5). When the pressure is reduced in the radiator by running off water, the spring will restore the seal to its seat on top of the radiator. When the radiator cools its coolant pressure decreases. Air pressure on the outside forces the vacuum seal (7) against the pressure of the vacuum spring (8) to allow air to pass through the seal into the radiator.

Failure of the pressure cap causes overheating and boiling over. The operating pressure of the cap can be tested with a pressure gauge and the condition of the seal can be inspected visually.

Sealed system

To prevent the loss of water, and hence the need for topping up the radiator, a sealed system is sometimes used. An overflow tank is fitted on the side of the radiator and a rubber tube from the pressure cap connects to the overflow tank. Thus any water allowed past the radiator can go into the overflow tank. When the radiator cools and water contracts, the water in the overflow tank is drawn into the radiator to fill the space available.

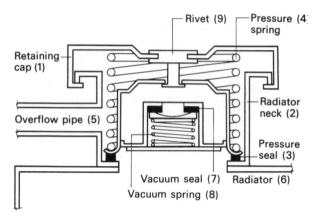

Radiator pressure cap

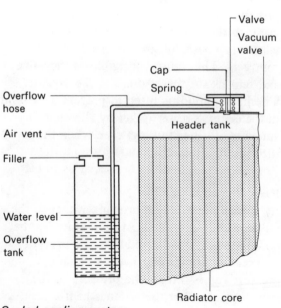

Sealed cooling system

Hoses

Rubber hoses are used to connect the engine
to the radiator. The radiator is attached to the
chassis whilst the engine is free to move in its
mountings. The rubber hoses allow an amount
of flexibility. They are made from a textile
fabric coated on both the inside and the
outside with rubber. Flexing of the hoses can
cause them to deteriorate: cracks eventually
leads to breakages, which cause loss of water.
The hoses are held in place with clips which
are tightened up with a screwdriver.

Replacing a hose

To replace a hose the water should first be
drained by undoing the drain tap. Then the
screws on the clips are slackened and the hose
pulled off the stubs on the radiator and the
engine. To remove the hose, loosen the clip by
turning the slotted part anti-clockwise. A new
hose can be fitted by using the reverse
procedure. Before fitting a new hose the stubs
should be cleaned with emery cloth. A fixing
cement can be used if needed.

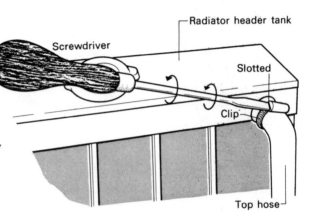

Changing a radiator hose

Anti-freeze

Anti-freeze is added to the cooling water to
prevent the radiator freezing in cold weather,
i.e. below 0°C. The chemical generally used is
ethylene glycol. For average European winters
a $33\frac{1}{3}\%$ solution of anti-freeze is used, i.e.
one-third anti-freeze to two-thirds water. The
best method is to mix these before pouring
into the radiator. The amount of anti-freeze
can be checked by using a special hydrometer.

Air-cooling system

Air-cooling systems are used on certain light cars and most motor cycles. Air cooling has the advantages of not using water and needing less moving parts. Having no water, it cannot freeze or leak. However, air-cooled engines tend to be more noisy than water-cooled ones. The system operates by air entering through the flap valve. The fan, which is driven by a crankshaft pulley, forces the air over the fins of the cylinder. The air is then discharged back into the atmosphere. The flap valve is controlled by the thermostat, which opens the flap when the engine is hot, so allowing air in. The flap is closed when the engine is cold, so restricting air flow and allowing the engine to warm up quickly.

Fan Belt

A V-shaped fan belt, sometimes called a 'V' belt, is used to drive the fan, the water pump and generator. It is important that the belt is free from cracks and shredding. It must be adjusted to give between 10 and 20 mm ($\frac{1}{2}$-to $\frac{3}{4}$-inch) free play. This is done by moving the generator on its mounting bracket, and an elongated adjustment is provided for this purpose. The fan-belt adjustment is made on the longest run of the belt by pulling and pushing gently with finger and thumb.

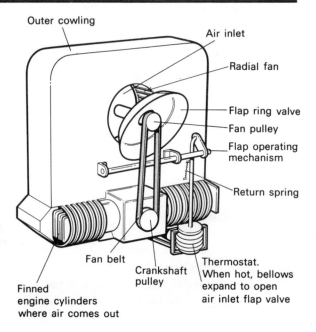

Air-cooling system

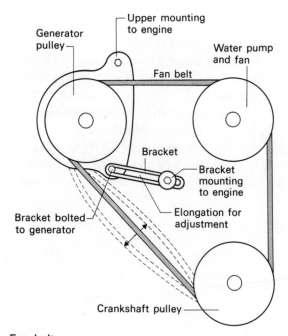

Fan belt

Multiple-choice questions

1 The normal operating temperature of a car engine is approximately:
(a) 185°C
(b) 32°C
(c) 20°C
(d) 85°C

2 The component which gives a quick warm-up and keeps the engine at a constant temperature is the:
(a) radiator
(b) water pump
(c) thermostat
(d) pressure cap

3 A cross-flow radiator may be found in a:
(a) sports car
(b) commercial vehicle
(c) bus
(d) estate car

4 Two advantages of the air cooling system are:
(a) it is cheap and easy to clean
(b) it uses no water and has few moving parts
(c) it is relatively quiet and does not freeze-up
(d) it is cheap and quiet

5 The component which circulates water in a cooling system is the:
(a) radiator
(b) distributor
(c) thermostat
(d) water pump

6 To prevent the cooling system from boiling over at high altitudes, which component is fitted:
(a) hoses
(b) pressure cap
(c) thermostat
(d) water jacket

7 To give the hoses flexibility they are made from:
(a) steel
(b) copper
(c) rubber
(d) aluminium

8 The advantage of a sealed cooling system is:
(a) less topping-up is required
(b) less water is needed
(c) no air is needed
(d) no anti-freeze is needed

9 A $33\frac{1}{3}$ percent anti-freeze solution means one part of anti-freeze to how many parts of water:
(a) 3
(b) 2
(c) 4
(d) 1

10 The component which drives the water pump, fan and generator is the:
(a) 'F' belt
(b) 'V' belt
(c) timing chain
(d) clutch

6 The clutch

The purpose of the clutch is to transmit the torque, or turning force, from the engine to the transmission. It is designed so that the drive can be engaged and disengaged smoothly and easily. By disengaging the drive, the clutch allows the gears to be changed smoothly and it provides a temporary neutral position. This allows the transmission gears to be engaged or disengaged whilst the engine is running.

The clutch assembly is contained in the bell-housing between the engine and the gearbox. The main components of the clutch are the pressure plate, the spinner plate and the flywheel. Engagement and disengagement are carried out by means of a footpedal-operated mechanism.

There are two types of pressure plates, each of which operate differently: the coil-spring pressure plate and the diaphragm-spring pressure plate. Both types look similar from the outside. The coil-spring pressure plate is deeper than the diaphragm-spring plate, and on close inspection the different components can be seen inside.

Transmission of torque

The transmission of torque from the engine to the gearbox depends on the strength of the springs in the pressure plate and the diameter of the spinner plate. The stronger the springs and the larger the diameter of the spinner plate, the greater the torque which can be transmitted. The clutches of HGVs are up to three times the diameter of those on private cars, and they can weigh about ten times more.

Coil-spring clutch
The pressure plate assembly is attached to the flywheel with set screws so that it turns with the engine. The *pressing plate*, fitted inside the pressure plate, holds the spinner plate against the flywheel by the pressure of the coil springs. The pressing plate is attached to the cover of the pressure plate with either straps or protrusions into eyes, so that the pressing plate and the springs revolve with the engine. The spinner plate, which is clamped between the pressing plate and the flywheel, also rotates. The centre of the spinner plate is splined, and the input shaft from the gearbox

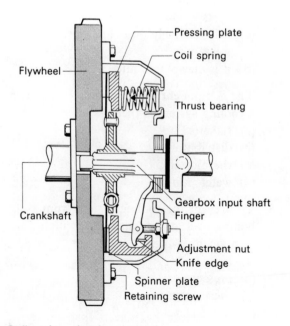

Coil-spring clutch engaged

is slid into the splines in the spinner plate so that the input shaft turns with the spinner plate. Therefore when the engine rotates, the gearbox input shaft also rotates.

To disengage the clutch the thrust race is pushed forwards by one of various types of mechanisms (see later). The thrust race pushes the inner end or free end of the fingers forwards. There are usually three fingers to give even clutch operation, and these pivot on adjustable pivots so that their opposite ends move backwards, so forcing the pressing plate backwards away from the spinner plate against the spring pressure. Taking the pressure off the spinner plate allows it to spin freely between the flywheel and the pressing plate. This disconnects the drive between the engine and the gearbox.

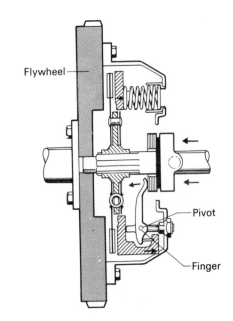

Coil-spring clutch disengaged

Diaphragm-spring clutch

The diaphragm-spring clutch has the following advantages over the coil spring clutch with equivalent performance:

1 It is smaller, having one flat spring.
2 It is lighter, having less metal in it.
3 It has less moving parts to go wrong or wear.
4 Its operation is consistently smooth, having only one spring.

In the engaged position the diaphragm spring is shaped rather like a saucer. The force of the outer rim forces the pressing plate against the spinner plate. The contruction of the cover and the pressing plate is very much like those of a coil spring clutch. The cover is bolted to the flyweel and the pressing plate is connected to the cover with flexible metal straps. Thus the pressing plate and diaphragm springs rotate with the flywheel. The diaphragm spring pivots on the cover with shouldered rivets. It is against these rivets that the spring forces itself to transmit pressure to the

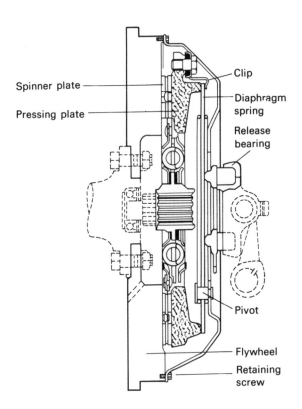

Diaphragm-spring clutch engaged

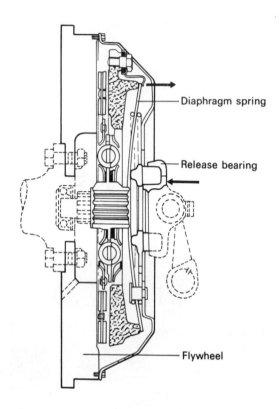

Diaphragm-spring clutch disengaged

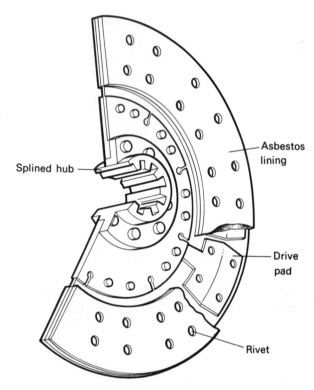

Clutch (friction disc); solid-centre spinner plate

pressing plate and the flywheel to transmit the drive.

To disengage the clutch the thrust race presses the diaphragm spring in the middle. This causes it to turn on the rivets and lift its outer rim. The lifting of the outer rim pulls the pressing plate away from the spinner plate, so allowing the spinner plate to rotate freely, disengaging the drive between the engine and the gearbox. The spinner plate and input shaft are the same with both coil- and diaphragm-spring clutches.

Spinner plate
The spinner plate consists of a steel hub which fits on the splines of the gearbox input shaft. Attached to the hub is a disc which carries the friction material, a mixture of asbestos and

resin. This material has a high coefficient of friction, coupled with good wearing properties and a natural resistance to burning. The friction material is riveted onto the disc of the spinner plate.

Safety note
Asbestos is a dangerous material. The inhalation of asbestos dust can lead to cancer of the lung.

There are two types of spinner plate in common use: the *solid-centre* type and the *spring-centre* type. In the diagram it can be seen that the drive between the asbestos lining and the splined centre is solid and has no give. Also shown is a sprung-centre spinner plate, in which the drive from the friction material on the outer section is transmitted to the splined

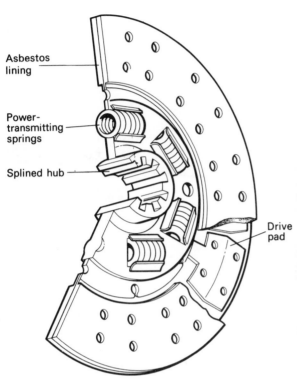

Asbestos
lining

Power-
transmitting
springs

Splined hub

Drive
pad

*Clutch (friction disc); sprung-centre spinner
plate*

hub through springs. The springs serve two
purposes:

1 They absorb shock loads when the clutch is
engaged suddenly.
2 They absorb the small fluctuations in
engine speed and vibrations, giving a
smooth transmission of power to the road.

Clutch-release bearing mechanism

Operating mechanisms

The clutch is engaged and disengaged with the
left-hand pedal. The pedal can be connected to
the thrust race assembly by one of several
methods: rod, cable or hydraulic.

Rod clutch
The rod method of operation is the simplest,
as can be seen in the diagram. A steel rod is
connected between the pedal and the clutch
cross-shaft. When the clutch pedal is depressed
the rod is pulled and the cross-shaft rotated.
The clutch cross-shaft transmits the movement
from the rod (or cable) to the thrust bearing,
which presses on the pressure plate to
disengage the clutch. This type of clutch is not
common, as any engine vibrations are

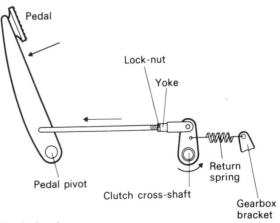

Pedal

Lock-nut

Yoke

Pedal pivot

Clutch cross-shaft

Return
spring

Gearbox
bracket

Rod clutch

transmitted through the rod to the clutch
pedal. Therefore the cable clutch has
superseded it.

Cable clutch

The cable clutch, is used on a large proportion
of small and medium-sized cars. An inner
cable travels inside an outer cable, or sheaf, as
it is sometimes called. The inner cable pulls
the clutch cross-shaft round in the same way
as the rod clutch. The cable, however, does
not transmit the vibrations of the gearbox to
the engine, so it is quieter and easier to
operate.

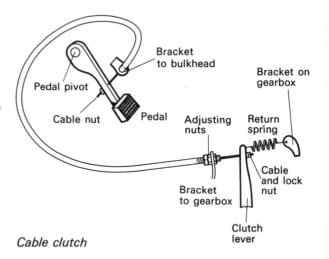

Cable clutch

Hydraulic clutch

Both the rod and the cable clutches rely on
mechanical linkages and therefore on the
lengths of the levers for their mechanical
advantage. A more sophisticated system is the
hydraulic clutch. This uses hydraulic fluid,
like that used in hydraulic brakes, to transmit
the movement from the clutch pedal to the
clutch cross-shaft in the bell-housing. This
system has its mechanical advantage (the
difference between the pressure applied by the
foot on the pedal and the actual pressure
moving the clutch thrust race) built into the
hydraulic system.

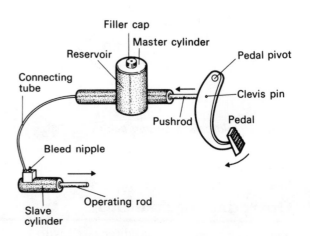

Hydraulic clutch

The clutch pedal moves a pushrod which
pushes a hydraulic piston into the master
cylinder. The hydraulic fluid above the piston
is forced along the connecting tube. This fluid
in turn forces the slave cylinder piston against
the operating rod which moves the clutch
cross-shaft. These systems are very efficient
and smooth in operation, being used on large
cars and trucks. It is essential that the fluid in
the master cylinder reservoir is kept topped up
to the right level.

Faults and adjustments

The main faults likely to occur to a clutch are *slipping* and *grabbing*. Slipping occurs when drive is not transmitted and can be brought about by:

1 Fatigued springs.
2 Oil on the friction lining.
3 Worn friction lining.
4 Wrong adjustment.

Grabbing occurs when the clutch cannot be engaged smoothly. It suddenly grabs and takes up the drive with a thud. Grabbing can be brought about by:

1 Uneven spring wear.
2 Damaged components.
3 Wrong adjustment.

The adjustment is made by screwing the adjustment nuts on the rod or cable. Hydraulic systems are usually self-adjusting. The adjustment is made so that there is about 2 mm free play at the end of the operating arm. This can be double-checked in the car by measuring the free play at the pedal. There should be about 25 mm (1 inch) free play at the pedal.

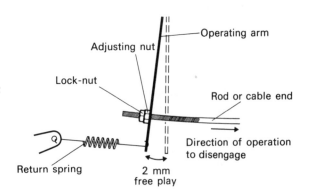

Clutch adjustment

Multiple-choice questions

1 *Rod*, *cable* and *hydraulic* are all types of:
   (a) clutch plate
   (b) clutch mechanism
   (c) bell housing
   (d) gearbox

2 The clutch which is the lightest, most compact and has the least moving parts is the:
   (a) multi-spring clutch
   (b) coil-spring clutch
   (c) diaphragm clutch
   (d) wet clutch

3 *Solid-centre* and *spring-centre* are both types of:
   (a) diaphragm
   (b) pressure plate
   (c) release bearing
   (d) spinner plate

4 The clutch friction lining is made from:
   (a) asbestos
   (b) aluminium
   (c) steel
   (d) carbon

5   If there is 2 mm play at the clutch lever,
the amount of play at the clutch pedal
will be:
(a) 25 mm
(b) 10 mm
(c) 50 mm
(d) 20 mm

6   Rod and cable adjustment are achieved
by:
(a) spring movement
(b) collets
(c) bleeding
(d) nut and locknut

7   The function of the clutch is to:
(a) smoothly engage and disengage the
     drive
(b) transmit the drive to the road wheels
(c) transmit the drive to the propeller
     shaft
(d) turn the gearbox

8   *Fingers*, *strips* and *eyes* are found in the:
(a) diaphragm
(b) coil spring pressure plate
(c) friction disc
(d) release mechanism

9   The clutch spinner plate is splined to the:
(a) output shaft
(b) layshaft
(c) clutch pedal
(d) input shaft

10   Oil on the friction lining, or a worn
friction lining, will cause:
(a) noise
(b) sliding
(c) slipping
(d) grabbing

7 The gearbox

Layout and function

The gearbox is fitted behind the engine and clutch on conventional layout vehicles. The bell-housing which covers the clutch is usually part of the gearbox casing and connects the gearbox to the engine. On conventional cars a ring of bolts secures the gearbox to the engine around the bell-housing. The weight of the gearbox is supported at the rear with a cross-member which attaches the gearbox to the chassis. The gearbox is supported on the cross-member with rubber mountings to give flexibility. With the rubber engine mountings they give the engine and gearbox unit some flexibility so that undue vibrations are not passed onto the vehicle's body and passengers.

Layout

The power enters the gearbox through the input shaft which is splined at its outer end into the clutch-driven plate. The power is passed through the constant-mesh gears to the lay shaft, then through the selected gear sets to the output shaft (see diagram). The output shaft is connected to the propeller-shaft which transmits the power or turning force onto the gear axle.

The gearbox casing is generally made from cast iron. It holds the gears firmly in place in relation to each other and provides a bath or container for the lubricating oil. Many of the parts of the gearbox have alternative names. Some only apply to different types of gearbox, whilst others vary with the manufacturers or the area concerned. The alternative names for the shafts are:

Input shaft: first motion shaft, primary shaft, clutch shaft, spigot shaft or jack shaft;
Lay shaft: second motion shaft or counter shaft;
Output shaft: mainshaft, third motion shaft.

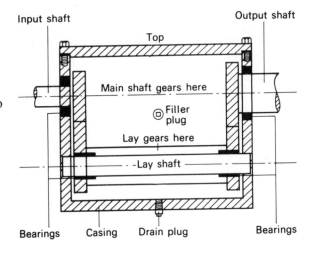

Basic layout of gearbox

Function

The gearbox is fitted to allow the car to accelerate and climb hills easily, and to reverse. This is done by using a selection of gear trains which enable changes to be made in the ratio of engine speed to wheel speed and, in the case of reverse gear, the direction of rotation.

The reason for needing a gearbox is that the engine only develops usable power over a limited range of engine speeds. The speeds at which the power is developed depends on the type of engine. For example, lorries develop their power at low engine speeds (about 2000 rpm) and racing cars at very high engine speeds (about 10 000 rpm). Modern cars and vans develop their usable power between 2000 and 5000 rpm. This means that if only one gear were fitted to the gearbox then, to be able to set off from rest, this gear would give about 15 km/h (10 mph) at 2000 rpm. It would give a top speed of $37\frac{1}{2}$ km/h (25 mph) corresponding to the first gear in a modern car. At the other end of the scale, if the top speed were to be 150 km/h (90 mph) at 5000 rpm the speed at 2000 rpm would be 60 km/h (36 mph), this being like top gear on many cars.

The gearbox acts as a lever, enabling a small engine to be able to move a very heavy object, acting like a tyre lever or crowbar. The gearbox also provides a means of reversing the car and a neutral position.

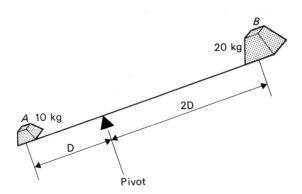

Gear ratio showing lever principle

Summing up the functions of the gearbox, they give:
1   Low gears for acceleration, moving heavy loads and climbing steep gradients.
2   High gears to enable high-speed cruising.
3   A neutral gear, so that the engine can be running whilst the car is stationary.
4   A reverse gear so that the car can be manoeuvered into parking spaces, garages, etc.

Gear ratio

The gear ratio of any two meshing gears is found by the formula

$$\text{Gear ratio} = \frac{\text{Number of teeth on driven gear}}{\text{Number of teeth on driver gear}}$$

This is usually written $= \dfrac{\text{driven}}{\text{driver}}$

Where two gears mesh together (see diagram) the gear ratio is:

$$\frac{B}{A} = \frac{50}{25} = \frac{2}{1}$$

This is written 2:1 (said 2 to 1).

This means that for each two turns of A, B will rotate one turn: hence two (turns) to one (turn), i.e. the gear B will rotate at half the speed of gear A. In other words, B will rotate at half the number of revolutions per minute compared with gear A.

If equal-size pulleys and ropes were attached to the shafts to which gears A and B are fixed, as in the diagram, it would be possible to use the 10 kg (22 lb) weight to raise the 20 kg (44 lb) weight. This is because the turning effort, or torque, is increased proportionally to the gear ratio. Although the speed is halved,

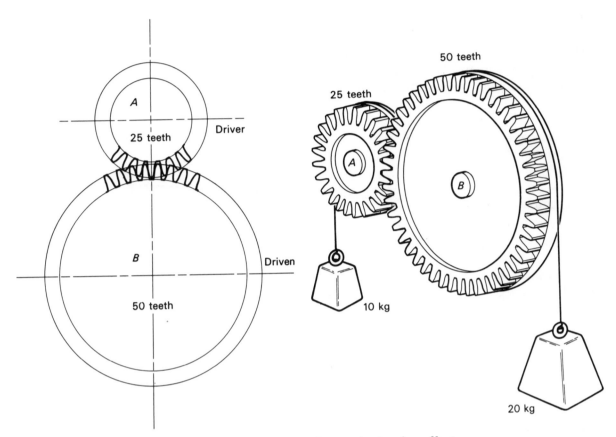

Gear ratio

Gear ratio: turning effort

the turning effort is doubled. This effect of the gear ratio is used when climbing steep hills or pulling heavy loads such as a trailer.

The gears used in a typical gearbox are in compounded sets of gears. For example, in first gear four gear wheels are in mesh and transferring the power from the clutch to the propeller-shaft. An example of this is shown in the diagram, with the input gear *A* and the two gears on the lay shaft *B* and *C* and the ouput gear *D*. By using more gear wheels in a compound train, smaller wheels can give a bigger ratio whilst taking up less space.

To calculate the gear ratio in the diagram we have to decide which are driven and which are driver gears. As *A* is the gear which gives the

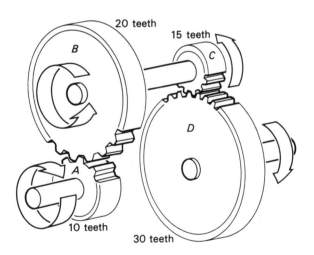

Compound gears

input this is a driver; gear *B* is driven by *A*.
Gear *C* is attached to the lay shaft like *B* and,
turning at the same speed, it is therefore a
driver to *D*, which must be driven. To
calculate these ratios they are multiplied
together:

$$\text{Gear ratio} = \frac{\text{Driven}}{\text{Driver}} \times \frac{\text{Driven}}{\text{Driver}}$$

In this case

$$\text{Gear ratio} = \frac{B}{A} \times \frac{D}{C}$$

If the number of teeth on each wheel were
A = 10, *B* = 20, *C* = 15 and *D* = .30 the
formula would become

$$\text{Gear ratio} = \frac{20}{10} \times \frac{30}{15} = \frac{600}{150} = \frac{4}{1}$$

Therefore the gear ratio is 4:1.

Gear teeth

There are three types of gears in use: *spur
gear*, *helical gear* and *double helical gear*. Each
kind of gear can be identified by the shape of
its teeth.

Spur gear
The spur gear has straight gear teeth.
Sometimes the teeth are referred to as being
straight cut. The straight gear teeth can only
carry a limited load and they are also noisy in
operation.

Spur gear

Helical gear
The helical gear, as its name suggests, has
helical-shaped teeth, i.e. the shape of the teeth,
if continued, would form a helix. An example
of a helix is the thread on a bolt. Being longer
for a given width of gear wheel, helical teeth
are stronger than straight cut ones. They are

Helical gear

also quieter in operation. Helical gears are used for most of the gears in a modern car's gearbox. However, the helical gear does have a disadvantage, i.e. side-thrust. The greater the load placed on two meshing helical gear teeth the greater the side-thrust which tends to part them. To overcome this problem, thrust bearings are used to hold them into mesh.

Double helical gear

The double helical gear has two rows of helical teeth. The two rows oppose each other, so that the side-thrust from one row is balanced by the side-thrust from the other row. Hence the gear overall gives little, if any, side-thrust. The double helical gear is used in the gearboxes of HGVs where high loads are carried.

Double helical gear

Epicyclic gears

In certain specialised gearboxes such as preselector and various types of automatic gearboxes, epicyclic gears are used. In the diagram the inner gear is called the sun gear (1), the outer toothed part is the annulus gear (2), and the small gears between the sun and the annulus are called planet gears (3). Various ratios can be obtained from one set of epicyclic gears by locking each section in turn to the gearbox casing. For example, in an automatic gearbox the annulus can be held by a brake band so that the power is transmitted from the sun gear to the planet gears. In this case, the planet gear are turning, i.e. running around the inside of the annulus. If the carrier of the planet gears is held, the sun will rotate the planets on their spindles, which will turn the annulus. The latter gear ratio would be the lower.

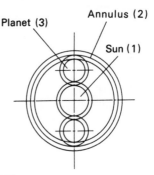

Epicyclic gear

This system of gearing is very compact, and offers much potential in automatic gearboxes and overdrive units. However, it is very expensive and needs great care in assembly.

Gearbox operation

There are two types of manual gearboxes in current use, the *sliding-mesh* gearbox and the *constant-mesh* gearbox. The sliding-mesh gearbox is so called because the gears slide into mesh with each other. The constant-mesh gears get their name from being constantly in mesh with each other. The alternative name for the sliding-mesh gearbox is the crash gearbox. The constant-mesh gearbox is called synchromesh, from its use of a synchromesh hub unit.

Sliding-mesh gearbox

The general layout of a sliding-mesh gearbox is shown in the diagram. The power enters the input shaft from the clutch. This turns the input gear, which in turn turns the layshaft. The input gear and the layshaft gear which turns with it are called constant-mesh gears. The power is transmitted to the main shaft from the layshaft by whichever main shaft gear is slid into contact. The engagement of each gear is detailed individually below and the

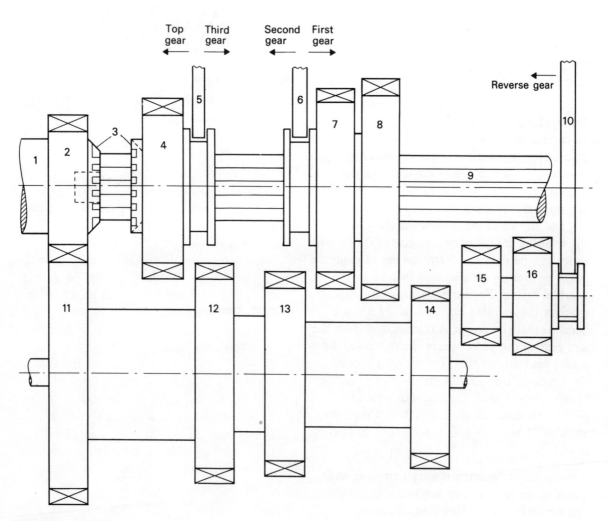

Four-speed sliding-mesh gearbox

numbers correspond to those in the diagram.

First gear
First gear on the mainshaft (8), is slid into mesh with the first gear on the layshaft (14). So the power from the input gear (2) goes to the layshaft (11), then from the first gear on the layshaft (14) to first gear on the mainshaft (8) (or output shaft, as it is also called). The sliding gears are splined on to the shaft mainshaft (9) so that the shaft turns when the gears are turned.

Second gear
Second gear on the mainshaft (7) is usually connected to first gear (8) so that only one selector fork (6) is needed to engage both first and second gears. This is done by pulling one way for first gear and the opposite for second gear. The second gear on the mainshaft (7) is slid along into mesh with second gear on the layshaft (13) so that the power path is input gear (2) to layshaft (11), second gear layshaft (13) to second gear mainshaft (7), through the splines to the mainshaft (9).

Third gear
Third gear is engaged by meshing the third gear on the mainshaft (4) with the third gear on the layshaft (12). So the power path is input gear (2) to layshaft (11), third gear (12) to mainshaft third gear (4) and that turns the mainshaft (9).

Fourth gear
Fourth gear is engaged by meshing the dog teeth (3) on the front of the third gear mainshaft (4) with those on the input gear (2). The top gear is therefore direct drive. The input shaft turns the mainshaft (9) at the same speed, the drive being through the dog teeth (3). The constant mesh gears (2 and 11) turn the layshaft, but it is only idling, as it is not transmitting any power. at all.

Reverse gear
Reverse gear is engaged by moving the reverse idler into mesh (15 and 16). The reverse idler is a shaft with two gears attached. One gear (16) meshes with the first gear on the layshaft, the other (15) with first gear on the main shaft. The power path is thus input gear to laygear to idler gear to first gear on the mainshaft. Looking at the front of the gearbox the gears and shafts will rotate in the directions as follows:

Input gear: clockwise
Layshaft gears: anti-clockwise
Reverse idler gear: clockwise
First gear and mainshaft: anti-clockwise

Neutral
When no gears are in mesh this is neutral, and in this position no drive is transmitted. However, the layshaft is always turned through the constant-mesh gears whenever the clutch is engaged.

Constant-mesh gearbox
All the gears, except reverse, are in constant mesh, not transmitting power but idling, except when engaged. The mainshaft gears are not splined to the mainshaft but run on bushes on the mainshaft. This means that the gears and the shaft can turn independently of each other. (See the diagram for the general layout.) To engage gear, the dog clutch units which are splined onto the mainshaft are slid into mesh with the dogs on the gears, so that the gear turns the dog clutch unit which transmits the power to the mainshaft. In modern gearboxes the synchromesh hub is used, and this is discussed later in this chapter. The power paths of each gear are detailed below, and the numbers refer to those given in the diagram.

Neutral
In neutral, no power is transmitted as no dog

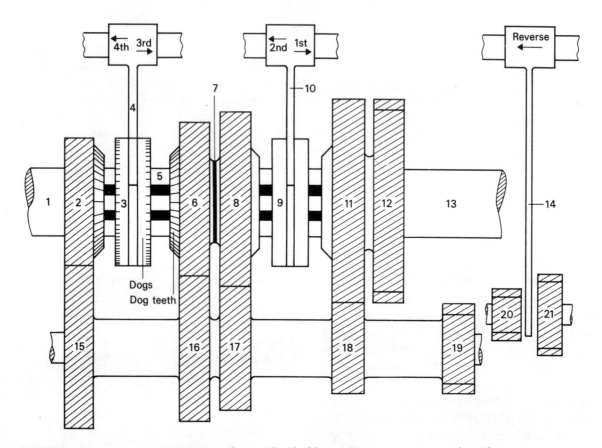

Four-speed constant-mesh gearbox. Gears 12, 19, 20 and 21 are spur gears, the others are helical gears

teeth are engaged. However, all the gears are turning when the engine is turning with the clutch engaged. The input gear turns the layshaft, as in the sliding-mesh gearbox. In this gearbox two gears are also called constant-mesh gears.

First gear
The dog clutch (9) is slid on the shaft (13) so that its teeth engage with those on the first gear mainshaft (11). The power path is then input gear (2) turns layshaft (15) which turns first gear on the mainshaft (11) through (18). The power then goes through the dogs to the dog clutch (9) and through the latter's splines to turn the mainshaft (13).

Second gear
The dog clutch unit (9) is slid in the opposite way to that to engage first so that its teeth are in mesh with those on second gear on the mainshaft (8). The power path is thus input gear (2) layshaft (15 and 17), second gear mainshaft (8), dog clutch (9), and mainshaft (13).

Third gear
The other dog clutch unit (3) is slid into mesh with the third gear on the mainshaft (6). The power path is similar to first and second gear, being input gear (2), layshaft (15 and 18), third gear mainshaft (6), dog clutch (3) and the mainshaft (13).

Fourth gear

Fourth gear is engaged by sliding the dog clutch unit (3) into mesh with the dog teeth on the input gear (2). This gives direct drive in the same way as the sliding-mesh gearbox, i.e. through the dog clutch splines to the mainshaft (13).

Reverse gear

Even in fully synchromesh gearboxes the reverse gear is engaged by sliding-gear methods. The idler gears (20 and 21) are slid into mesh with a reverse gear on the layshaft (19) and one on the mainshaft (12).

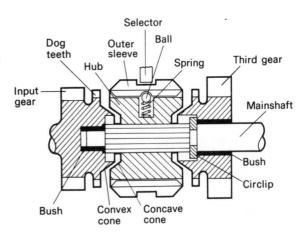

Synchromesh hub

Synchromesh hub

A synchromesh hub is shown in the diagram. It consists of a hub which is splined to the mainshaft and an outer sleeve which is splined to the hub. Spring-loaded balls hold the outer sleeve in the neutral or the engaged positions.

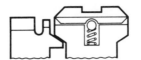 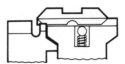

Synchromesh unit operation: initial interference of cones' synchronising speeds

Synchromesh unit operation: drive gear engaged; outer sleeve over dog teeth

When initial pressure is applied by the selector to the outer sleeve the pressure of the ball also moves the hub section. This causes the conical surface on the hub to give the initial interference to the cone on the gear involved. This interference adjusts the speeds of the mating shafts to the same speed, i.e. it synchronises them. Further pressure by the selector pushes the outer sleeve over the balls against the spring pressure until they engage in gear-engaged grooves. At this point the outer hub has engaged its inner splines with the outer dog teeth on the gear. Therefore the gear is fully engaged. Drive from the gear is passed from the dogs to the outer sleeve, to the hub and to the shaft.

Selector

The diagram shows a typical selector, or selector fork as it is more properly known. This is moved by a selector rod through a mechanism attached to the gear lever.

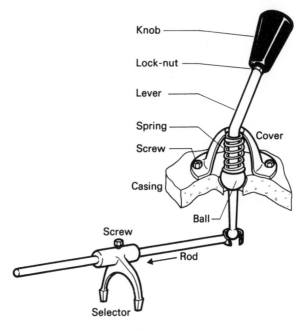

Gear lever mechanism

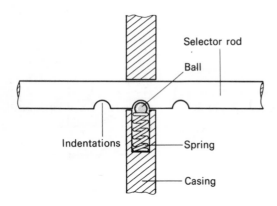

Gear selector detent

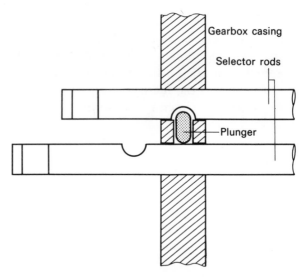

Selector detent

Detents

To ensure that the gears are held in whatever position is selected a system of detents is used, and examples are shown in the diagrams. The first and second diagrams show how springs and balls or plungers are used to hold the shaft in place. The C-shaped detent in the third diagram is a solid mechanical locking device.

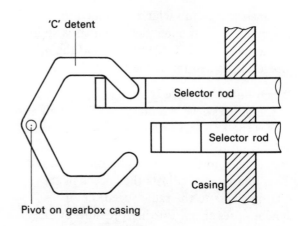

C-shaped detent (allows only one gear to be engaged at a time)

Gearbox removal

Removal of the gearbox is necessary to carry out clutch repairs as well as repairs to the gearbox itself. Most gearboxes are positioned underneath the vehicle, which means that a hoist or a pit is needed to remove them. The gearbox is held in place by the cross-member mounting and the ring of bolts around the bell-housing. Before attempting to remove the gearbox it is necessary to remove the propeller-shaft, the speedometer drive cable, the gear lever and the clutch-operating linkage. As the gearbox mounting usually forms a rear-engine mounting, it is necessary to support the rear of the engine before unbolting the cross-member.

(a) Stage 3—The inside of the gearbox

(b) Stage 6—The bell-housing is removed

(c) Stage 7—Input shaft, gear and bearing are withdrawn

(d) Stage 8—The mainshaft can now be withdrawn

Stripping

The method of stripping down varies from gearbox to gearbox. The diagrams show some common procedures.

The sequence of operation is as follows:

1 The gear lever mechanism is removed.
2 The gear selectors in the cover are removed.
3 The inside of the gearbox can now be seen.
4 The tail flange is removed.
5 The tail-housing is removed.
6 The bell-housing is removed.
7 The input shaft, gear and bearing are withdrawn.
8 The third and fourth synchromesh hubs are taken off the mainshaft. The mainshaft can now be withdrawn and the layshaft seen.

Lubrication

Various types of lubricant are used in modern gearboxes, and use of the same multigrade oils as in the engine is becoming common practice, i.e. 20/50 SAE oils (SAE-Society of Automotive Engineers). However, it is important to check with the workshop manual or data sheet, as many vehicles use 80 or 90 SAE oils. The oil should be added so that it is level with the bottom of the filler plug or mark on the gearbox dipstick. Some vehicles, especially front-wheel drive ones, have their engine oil and gearbox oils combined.

Multiple-choice questions

1 The component which allows the car to climb steep hills and be reversed is the:
   (a) clutch
   (b) gearbox
   (c) rear axle
   (d) differential

2 The shaft which transmits the power from the clutch is the:
   (a) layshaft
   (b) drive shaft
   (c) input shaft
   (d) tap shaft

3 The input gear and first gear on the layshaft are called:
   (a) idler gears
   (b) constant mesh gears
   (c) lay gears
   (d) input gears

4 Helical gears are used in which type of gearbox:
   (a) synchromesh
   (b) sliding mesh
   (c) automatic
   (d) manual

5 Heavy goods vehicle gearboxes use:
   (a) straight cut gears
   (b) double helical gears
   (c) epicyclic gears
   (d) helical gears

6 The formula of finding the gear ratio is:
   (a) $\dfrac{\text{Driver}}{\text{Driver}}$ (c) $\dfrac{\text{Driver}}{\text{Driven}}$
   (b) $\dfrac{\text{Driven}}{\text{Driven}}$ (d) $\dfrac{\text{Driven}}{\text{Driver}}$

7 *Sleeve, hub, balls* and *springs* are found in the:
   (a) gear shaft
   (b) synchromesh hub
   (c) fourth gear
   (d) reverse pinion

8 Automatic gearboxes usually have:
   (a) epicyclic gears
   (b) straight cut gears
   (c) helical gears
   (d) no gears at all

9 On a conventional motor car the gearbox is usually removed from:
   (a) under the bonnet
   (b) under the boot
   (c) underneath the car
   (d) through the floor

10 The gearbox casing is usually made from:
   (a) steel
   (b) cast iron
   (c) copper
   (d) tin

8 The propeller-shaft

On conventional motor cars the gearbox is mounted to the engine and chassis, whereas the rear axle is mounted on the road springs. The function of the propeller-shaft is to transmit the drive from the rear of the gearbox to the rear axle, so propelling the car. The rear axle moves up and down with the road springs as the car goes over bumps (see diagram). This movement means that the angle of the propeller-shaft between the gearbox and the rear axle changes as the car moves along the road. To accommodate changes in angle, a moving joint is fitted at the ends of the propeller-shaft. As the rear axles moves up and down it also tends to rotate, i.e. its nose moves about in an arc, called the nose arc. As the axle rotates, the distance between the gearbox and the rear axle changes. To allow the propeller-shaft to increase and decrease in length to accommodate axle movements a sliding joint is fitted to the propeller-shaft. The sliding joint allows about 75 mm (3 inches) of variation in length of the propeller-shaft.

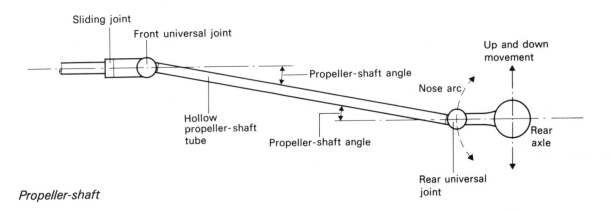

Propeller-shaft

Construction

The actual propeller-shaft is a hollow metal tube, each end being welded to a flange to accommodate the universal and sliding joints. A hollow tube is used because it is both light and strong.

Drive shafts
On rear-wheel drive (RWD) and front-wheel drive (FWD) vehicles, and vehicles with independent rear suspension (IRS), drive shafts are used to transmit the power from the differential to the driving wheels. The differential divides the drive between the two wheels, allowing the outer wheel to turn faster than the inner when cornering. These are like short propeller-shafts. As can be seen in the

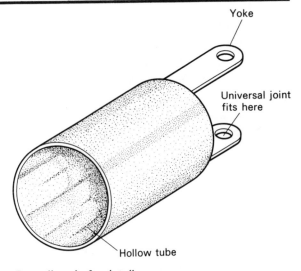

Propeller-shaft: detail

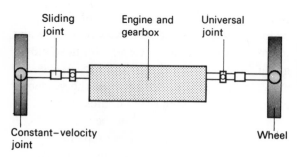

Layout of FWD drive shafts and joints

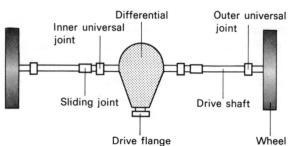

Layout of RWD (independent suspension) drive shafts

diagram for the FWD layout, the drive shaft contains a universal joint, a sliding joint and a constant-velocity joint. The constant-velocity joint is needed to ensure that the drive is transmitted evenly at all times. Also shown is an IRS layout. This, like the propeller-shaft, uses two universal joints and a sliding joint.

Types of universal joint
There are many types of universal joint in use; for example, the Hooke or Hardy Spicer joint, the Layrub coupling, the Rotaflex coupling, the fabric coupling and the Birfield joint. We will now look at each type of joint in turn and discuss their advantages and disadvantages.

Fabric coupling
The fabric coupling, sometimes known as the Hardy fabric coupling, has been used on many cars, lorries and motor cycles. It consists of a ring of canvas fabric bolted to the gearbox mounted flange on one side and the propeller-shaft flange on the other, the bolts fitting through the ring alternately. Being canvas, the joint cannot transmit much power. The joint does provide a cushion for the drive. However, undue shock loads will cause the joint to tear.

Rotaflex coupling
The Rotaflex coupling, often called the doughnut because of its shape, is a refined

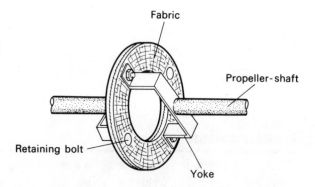

Fabric coupling

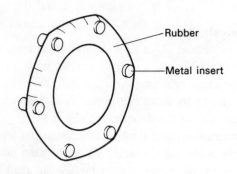

Rotaflex coupling

version of the fabric coupling. The Rotaflex coupling is a steel reinforced rubber ring, with six holes for fixing bolts, three to the drive flange and three to the shaft. The Rotaflex coupling is used mainly on the drive shafts of rear-wheel drive cars. The coupling is relatively large, so it needs quite a lot of space, which makes it unsuitable for FWD car drive shafts. Being rubber, it has the advantage of flexibility to cushion any shock loads from the drive. However, it also has the disadvantage of being perished by any oil which might stray onto it, which is the usual cause of failure of these joints. Rotaflex couplings can drive through an angle of about 15 degrees.

Layrub coupling

The Layrub coupling is a more sopisticated kind of joint. It is used on the propeller-shafts of both cars and lorries.

The shape is that of two saucers placed together rim to rim. The inside is filled with rubber. The bolts for attachment to the flanges pass through steel bushes going right through the joint. There can be four or six steel bushes. Being largely rubber, the joint absorbs shock loads and vibrations, giving an even transmission of power from the gearbox to the wheels. Again, being made of rubber also means that the joint can soon be perished by oil, although the outer metal casing makes the joint less vunerable than other types. The Layrub coupling is compact, light and flexible. The angle through which it can transmit drive is less than 15 degrees.

Hooke joint

The Hooke joint was invented by a physicist of that name (Robert Hooke, 1635–1703). Although the Hooke joint is its proper name it is known more popularly as a universal joint, and in the motor trade as a Hardy Spicer joint, the latter being the trade-name of the makers.

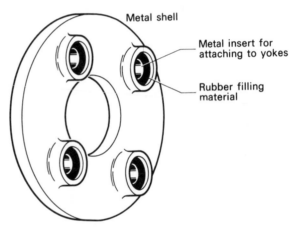

Metal shell

Metal insert for attaching to yokes

Rubber filling material

Layrub coupling

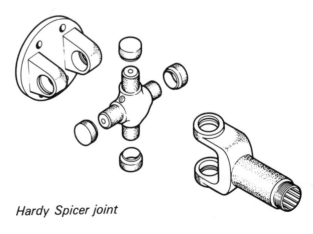

Hardy Spicer joint

The Hardy Spicer joint is constructed from a cruciform member which rotates in four cups each containing needle roller bearings (see diagram). Two of the cups fit into the gearbox or axle drive flange and two into the flange on the propeller-shaft. The needle roller bearings may be either pre-packed in a special grease or fitted with a grease nipple. The former type never needs greasing for the life of the bearing and the latter are greased at regular intervals. The normal service interval is 7500 km (5000 miles). In servicing, a grease gun is applied to the nipple and squeezed three or four times — over-lubricating can cause damage to the seals. Certain vehicles have Hardy Spicer joints fitted with a screw plug instead of a grease nipple. The plug should be removed every 15 000 km (10 000 miles) and a grease nipple screwed in whilst the joint is lubricated.

Hardy Spicer joints are fitted in pairs to give even transmission of power. The yokes must be fitted to the propeller-shaft in the same plane. Where a detachable sliding section is used it is often possible to fit them misaligned, which can lead to uneven running.

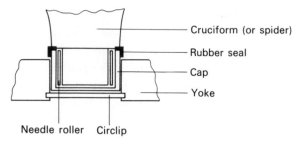

Cross-section through Hardy Spicer joint

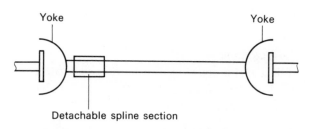

The yokes of the propeller-shaft fitted in the same plane

Birfield joint

To give constant velocity at the output of a single joint, a constant-velocity joint is used. This is the Birfield constant-velocity joint, which is used on many FWD vehicles such as the Mini, the Allegro and the Princess. Like the Hardy Spicer and other joints, it can transmit drive through an angle of about 15 degrees. Being compact, it is suitable for use on the drive shafts of FWD vehicles. It is usually fitted in-line with the swivel pin assembly. The drive is transmitted by ball bearings between the grooved inner and the outer members of the joint.

Sliding joint

The sliding joint is fitted to allow for the

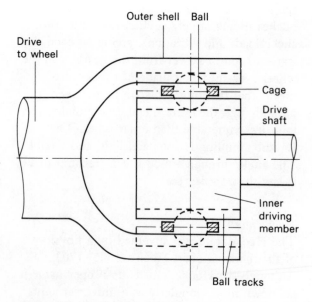

Ball driving joint (the Birfield constant-velocity joint has curved tracks)

change in distance between the gearbox and rear axle. This simply consists of splined inner and outer members. A locking ring is sometimes fitted to limit the amount of travel and to stop the two sections becoming parted. As with the Hardy Spicer joint, these can be pre-packed with special grease or lubricated through a grease nipple.

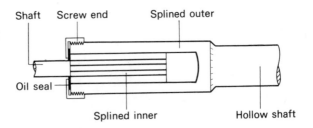

Propeller-shaft sliding joint

Support bearing

On very long vehicles it is often necessary to use two short propeller-shafts instead of one long one. This gives even transmission of power. To hold the inner ends of the propeller-shafts a support bearing is used. This is a rubber-mounted bracket, fitted with a bearing. It serves to hold the propeller-shafts firm and steady, which is especially important at high speeds. The support bearing is attached to the chassis between the gearbox and the rear axle.

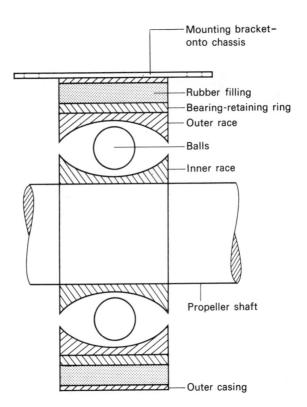

Propeller-shaft support bearing

Changing a joint

Most of the joints are held in place with nuts and bolts, so changing them is simply a matter of using the correct spanners, taking care to apply support where necessary. However, the Hardy Spicer joints require a special technique.

First, the propeller-shaft is removed and placed in a vice. The circlips are then removed from

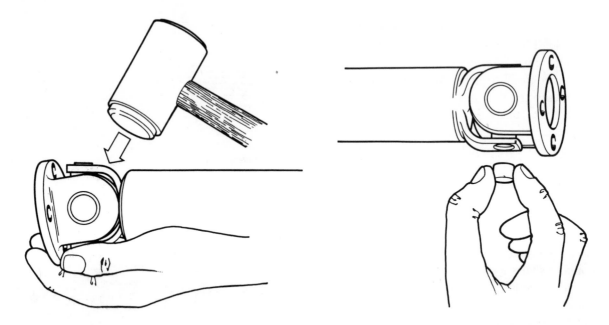

Changing a universal joint

underneath each cup. The side of the yokes are then hit until a cup pops up. The cup can then be withdrawn. This is done with the other cups, using the vice and a spacer to act as a press where necessary. The new joint is fitted by threading in the cruciform member and pressing home the new cups in the vice one at a time.

Multiple-choice questions

1 The sliding joint on the propeller shaft is fitted to:
    (a) allow for changes in angle
    (b) the Hardy Spicer
    (c) allow for changes in length
    (d) the Layrub

2 Universal Hardy Spicer joints have:
    (a) needle roller bearings
    (b) ball bearings
    (c) taper roller bearings
    (d) plain bearings

3 Constant velocity joints are usually found on:
    (a) PSV vehicles
    (b) conventional vehicles
    (c) FWD vehicles
    (d) RWD vehicles

4 The propeller shaft is made from:
    (a) square tube
    (b) round bar
    (c) iron pipe
    (d) hollow round tube

5 Robert Hooke invented a joint which is commonly known as the:
   (a) Hardy Spicer
   (b) Lay-rub
   (c) Rotaflex
   (d) C/V

6 *Cruciform*, *cups* and *needles* are found in the:
   (a) sliding joint
   (b) support bearing
   (c) Hooke type joint
   (d) Layrub

7 The rotaflex coupling is shaped like:
   (a) two saucers
   (b) a doughnut
   (c) a bun
   (d) a cross

8 The type of universal joint made from canvas is the:
   (a) Layrub
   (b) Hardy Spicer
   (c) Birfield
   (d) fabric coupling

9 Vehicles fitted with IFS and IRS always have:
   (a) drive shafts
   (b) half shafts
   (c) no propeller shaft
   (d) centre support bearings

10 On very long vehicles it is often necessary to use:
   (a) a long propeller shaft
   (b) Birfield joints
   (c) support bearing
   (d) two universal joints

9 The rear axle

A conventional rear axle is shown in the diagram. It carries inside it the following components:

1 Final drive gears.
2 Differential gear assembly.
3 Half-shafts.
4 Hubs and bearings.
5 Lubricating oil.

Rear axle assembly

Final drive gears

The final drive gears are made up of a crown wheel and a pinion. The pinion is the smaller gear, which is attached to the propeller-shaft by a bolted flange. The propeller-shaft turns the pinion at the same speed as the gearbox output shaft. The pinion is located in two bearings in the nose of the axle, i.e. the part which protrudes to the front of the casing. The crown wheel is so called because of its shape — it looks rather like a crown. The crown wheel is mounted onto the outside of the differential carrier. It is at right-angles to the pinion so the crown wheel and pinion turn the drive through 90 degrees — a right-angle. The final drive gears give the final drive gear ratio and determine the overall gear ratio.

Final drive gears

The final drive gear ratio is the ratio of the speed of the pinion to that of the crown wheel. As they are connected to the propeller-shaft and wheels, respectively, this is also the ratio between these components. The final drive gear ratio is found by the formula

$$\text{Final drive gear ratio} = \frac{\text{Number of teeth on crown wheel}}{\text{Number of teeth on pinion}}$$

For example, $\frac{50}{10} = \frac{5}{1}$

This is written 5:1 (said 5 to 1).

There are different types of gears used for the final drive gears: straight bevel gears, spiral bevel gears, hypoid bevel gears and the worm and wheel.

Straight bevel

Straight bevel gear teeth are shown in the diagram. This type of gear is not strong and is very noisy in operation. It set the pattern for the modern gears, but is not used on any current vehicles.

Spiral bevel

The spiral bevel gear was developed from the straight bevel gear. As can be seen from the diagram, it is curved, which means that each tooth is longer and therefore stronger. The spiral bevel is also quieter than its predecessor. The spiral bevel has been superseded by the hypoid bevel, but it was used extensively for many years.

Hypoid bevel

The pinion of the hypoid bevel gear assembly is set below the centre line of the crown wheel. This is unlike the straight and spiral bevel types, which have the centre line of their pinions in line with that of their crown wheels. Setting the pinion lower down gives the advantage of longer and quieter gear teeth. It also gives the secondary advantage of allowing a lower propeller-shaft which, in turn, gives a lower and flatter floor in the car. This is the most common type of final drive arrangement.

The offset of the pinion, i.e. the distance between the centre line of the pinion and the centre line of the crown wheel, is usually approximately one-fifth of the diameter of the crown wheel. It is usual to say that the offset is one fifth. By offsetting the pinion, the pinion diameter can be increased for a given size of crown wheel. Given one-fifth offset the

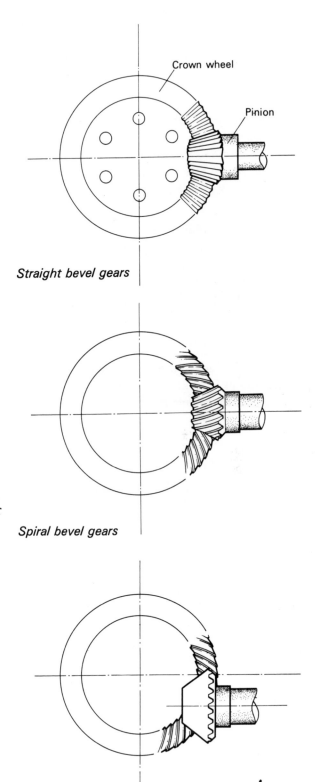

Straight bevel gears

Spiral bevel gears

Hypoid bevel gears

pinion can be 30% larger than when the centre lines are in the same plane. Therefore the pinion is much stronger and capable of carrying greater loads.

Should the gear teeth and the supporting bearings wear, it will be necessary to replace them. New items cannot just be bolted in, but it is necessary to set up the gear teeth so that they mesh together smoothly and silently.

Worm and wheel

The worm and wheel is an alternative to the more usual crown wheel and pinion. The worm replaces the pinion and the wheel replaces the crown wheel. The worm can be fitted above or below the wheel. This arrangement is used mainly on very heavy goods vehicles and some public service vehicles. The advantages of the worm and wheel are its very high load-carrying capacity and its ability to give a very low gear ratio.

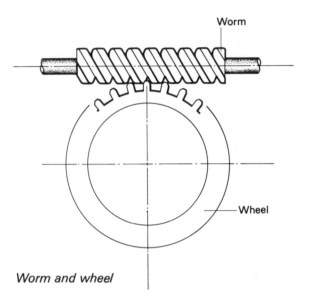

Worm and wheel

Differential

The differential gears are mounted inside a carrier on the outside of which is the crown wheel. The differential carrier is mounted in bearings onto the axle casing. The diagram shows a cross-sectional view of the differential assembly. The differential gear components comprise two sun-gear wheels which are attached to the half-shafts and two planet-gear wheels which are free to rotate on a cross-shaft attached to the carrier.

Functions of the differential

The functions of the differential are

1 To allow one wheel to turn faster than the other. For instance, when turning a corner the outer wheel will travel further, and hence faster, than the inner.

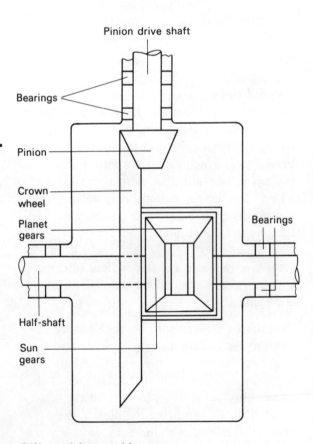

Differential assembly

2 To divide the driving force, or torque, evenly between both rear wheels.

Operation

The diagram shows the essential differential gears. Under normal straight-line conditions the pinion rotates the crown wheel which turns the differential carrier. The carrier turns bodily turning the planet gears; the planet gears do not rotate but pass the torque onto the sun gears which drive the wheels through the half-shafts. The speed and the turning force is the same for both wheels.

On cornering, the inner wheel drive-shaft and sun wheel is slowed, and the planet wheels rotate around the slowed sun gear, turning on their shaft. This movement is passed onto the outer sun wheel, which is thereby made to turn faster. The speed lost by one sun gear is gained by the other.

Half-shaft

The half-shaft connects the sun gear wheel to the hub, so transmitting the drive to the road wheel. The inner end is splined into the sun gear wheel, the outer end has a taper or flange assembly to connect to the hub.

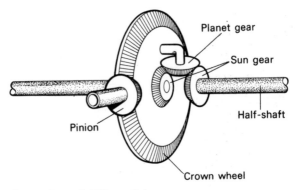

Operation of differential

Types of hub/axle assemblies

The rear hub/axle assembly is subjected to considerable forces, namely:

1 Driving force to the rear wheels.
2 Braking forces.
3 The load of the vehicle.

These forces put bending and shear stresses on the rear axle. To provide sufficient strength without undue weight, three types of hub/axle bearing arrangements are in use: *semi-floating*, *three-quarter floating* and *fully floating*.

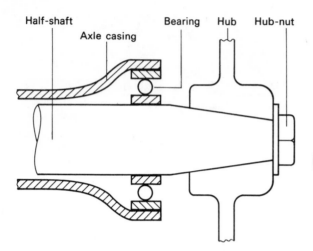

Semi-floating hub assembly (oil seals not shown)

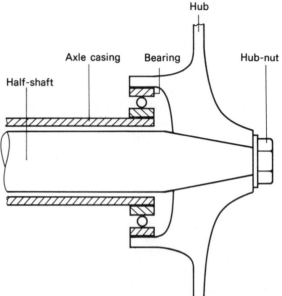

Semi-floating

The semi-floating assembly is the weakest arrangement as the bearing is between the inside of the axle casing and the half-shaft. This arrangement is used on many light cars to which it is well suited. However, should the half-shaft break, which is quite rare nowadays, the wheel is liable to fall off.

Three-quarter floating

The three-quarter floating arrangement is much stronger than the semi-floating type. The bearing is situated between the hub and axle casing. The three-quarter floating arrangement is used on heavy cars, light vans and pick-up trucks. The bulk of the weight of the car is supported by the bearing, hence the name three-quarter floating.

Fully floating

The half-shaft in this arrangement carries none of the vehicle's weight, hence the name fully floating. The hub is supported by twin ball or roller bearings. The fully floating arrangement is used on heavy goods vehicles and public service vehicles. The bearing arrangement leads to a wide and heavy rear axle, which is

Three-quarter floating hub assembly (oil seals not shown)

Note: oil seals are not shown

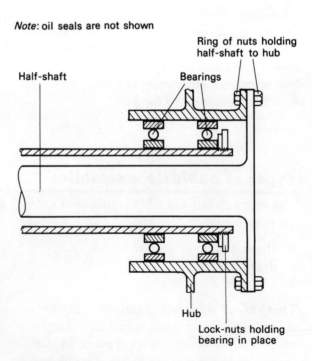

Fully floating hub assembly (oil seals not shown)

not a problem on HGVs and PSVs, but would be on a private car. The half-shaft on this layout can be changed without jacking up the vehicle.

Lubrication
The use of the correct lubricating oil in the rear axle is very important. The usual grade for cars is 90 SAE, but other grades are used. As well as the viscosity, the actual content of the oil is important. Hypoid oil contains a special mixture of sulphur to cope with the hypoid gear teeth. The oil should be kept topped up to the filler plug level, or dipstick mark. This should be checked every 7500 km (5000 miles).

Overall gear ratio

The overall gear ratio is found by multiplying the gearbox ratio by the rear axle ratio. The formula is:

$$\text{Overall gear ratio} = \text{Gearbox ratio} \times \text{rear anxle ratio}$$

Example
A car has a gearbox third gear ratio of 2:1 and a top gear ratio of 1:1. The rear axle ratio is 4:5:1. Find the overall gear ratio in both third and top gears.

1 Third overall gear ratio
= 2 × 4.5 = 9:1
2 Top overall gear ratio
= 1 × 4.5 = 4.5:1

Multiple-choice questions

1 The component which turns the drive through 90° and gives a gear reduction is the:
(a) differential
(b) rear hub
(c) final drive
(d) half shaft

2 The final drive gear ratio is found from the formula:
(a) no. of teeth on crown wheel / no. of teeth on pinion
(b) no. of teeth on pinion / no. of teeth on crown wheel
(c) no. of teeth on pinion / no. of teeth on differential
(d) no. of teeth on sun wheel / no. of teeth on planet wheel

3 The inner end of the half shaft is attached to the:
(a) sun gear
(b) planet gear
(c) hub
(d) crown wheel

4 Fully floating and three-quarter floating are types of:
(a) differential
(b) half shaft
(c) final drive
(d) hub/axle arrangement

5   The formula for the overall gear ratio is:
   (a) gearbox ratio × rear axle ratio
   (b) gearbox ratio × differential ratio
   (c) number of teeth on planet gear ×
       number of teeth on sun gear
   (d) driver × driven

6   The viscosity grade of axle oil is usually:
   (a) SAE 10
   (b) SAE 20/50
   (c) SAE 30
   (d) SAE 90

7   The component which allows one wheel
   to turn faster than the other whilst
   transmitting the driving torque equally is
   the:
   (a) final drive
   (b) half shaft
   (c) differential
   (d) hub

8   The axle casing is attached to the rear leaf
   springs with:
   (a) 'U' bolts
   (b) nuts and bolts
   (c) shackles
   (d) clips

9   The worm and wheel is used in the rear
   axle of:
   (a) sports cars
   (b) HGVs
   (c) estate cars
   (d) light vans

10 Hypoid bevel is a type of:
   (a) differential
   (b) hub
   (c) pinion flange
   (d) final drive

10 The suspension and steering

The front suspension and the steering are combined into one unit; the rear suspension is generally combined with the rear axle. On front-wheel drive vehicles the layout is more complicated, as the drive has to be turned through the steered angle. In this chapter we will look at the basic systems and common practices.

Function of suspension

The function of the suspension is to prevent the bumps caused by road-surface irregularities from reaching the occupants of the car. This makes the car pleasant to ride in and easy to drive. In the case of a goods vehicle the suspension protects the load from damage. Consider what it would be like in the back of an egg-delivery van if it were to have no suspension! The suspension also protects the mechanical components from vibration, so giving them a longer life.

The suspension, front or rear, consists of a system of movable linkages, a spring and a shock absorber. The pneumatic tyre also forms part of the suspension. The flexibility of the tyre serves to absorb small irregularities and reduce noise.

Function of steering

The steering is needed to guide the car along its chosen path, the principle being that the rear wheels will follow the front ones. The front wheels and their tyres must exert enough force on the road to overcome any tendency by the car to deviate from whatever course it is following. Steering the front wheels, i.e. turning them from side to side, is achieved by means of a system of rods and levers operated by the steering wheel through the steering box or rack and pinion unit.

Before we look at the actual methods of achieving suspension and steering we will define some of the terms used to describe the suspension design, i.e. castor, camber, king-pin inclination, Ackermann principle and toe-in/toe-out.

Castor
Castor, or, more fully, the *castor angle*, is the angle that the king-pin or swivel pin arrangement is angled backwards in the

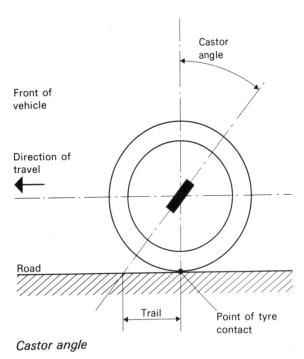

Castor angle

longitudinal plane. By giving the king-pin a certain amount of castor angle (about 1 or 2 degrees), the imaginary centre line hits the road before the centre of the wheel. This gives the wheel a self-aligning or self-centering action. The wheel follows the pivot, so keeping the car on a straight course and reducing the need to straighten the steering after negotiating a corner. This can be likened to the castors on a trolley, or piece of heavy furniture. The castors swing round so that the trolley can be pushed in a straight line.

Camber

Camber is the inclination of the road wheel in the transverse plane. The wheel is generally inclined outwards at the top, and this is called *positive camber*. Negative camber is the term used when the wheel is inclined inwards at the top.

King-pin inclination

King-pin inclination (KPI) is the inclination of the king-pin in the transverse plane, i.e. the same plane as wheel camber but at 90 degrees to the castor angle. Normally the king-pin is inclined inwards at the top by about 1 degree. This is called positive KPI. Negative KPI is when the king-pin is inclined outwards at the top. So positive KPI is an inclination opposite to positive camber, and this gives centre-point steering: the meeting of camber and KPI centre lines in the middle of the patch where the tyre meets the road.

Ackermann principle

When a vehicle turns a corner all its wheels must rotate about a common point. This can perhaps be better imagined if the vehicle is thought to be going round in a full circle; all the wheels must be turning about the centre point of that circle. This is achieved by taking radius lines from the centres of the wheels and turning the wheels so that they are tangential

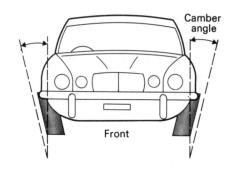

Camber angle

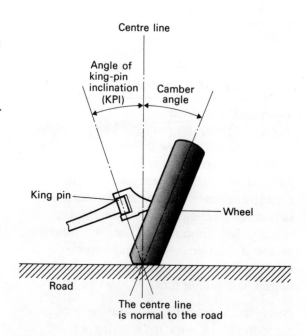

King-pin inclination (KPI)

to the radius lines. As the diagram shows, the two rear wheels are on the same radius line as they cannot be steered separately. The steered wheels are on separate axes. This means that the steering mechanism has to be designed so that the inner wheel is always turned through

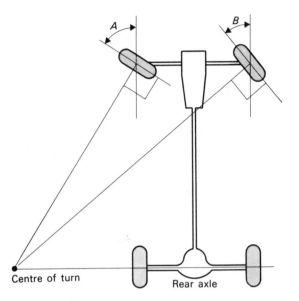

Ackermann principle

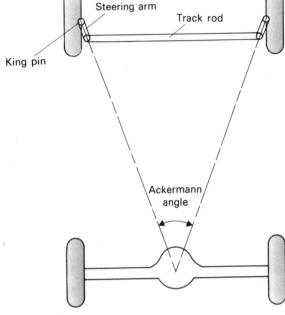

a greater angle than the outer. In the diagram, *A* and *B* are the angles through which the wheels have to be turned. The inner angle, *A*, is greater than the outer, *B*.

Ackermann angle

Ackermann's system of inclining the steering arms inwards so that their centre lines meet at or just before the rear axle gives this effect. This is referred to as the Ackermann angle or principle and the diagram shows a typical system. As this principle is difficult to understand I suggest that the student makes a cardboard model of these linkages to observe their action in operation.

Toe-in and toe-out
On most cars the front wheels are aligned so that they *toe-in,* i.e. the front of the wheels are closer together than the rear. The toe-in is usually set at about 2 mm.

On front-wheel drive vehicles and certain other specialised cars and trucks the wheel alignment is set to *toe-out*. Again this is usually about 2 mm.

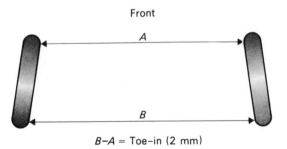

$B-A$ = Toe-in (2 mm)

Toe-in

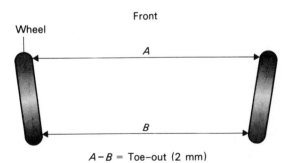

$A-B$ = Toe-out (2 mm)

Toe-out

Beam axle suspension

The original type of suspension which is still
used on many light vans as well as HGVs and
PSVs is the beam axle and leaf spring system.
A beam goes transversly across the vehicle.
The axle is connected to the chassis with leaf
springs. The leaf spring consists of a main leaf
which has an eye at each end and several other
supporting leaves. This, like most other
suspension and steering components, is made
from medium-carbon steel. The front eye of
the spring is attached to the chassis with a
fixed shackle; the rear eye has a swinging
shackle. The spring is attached to the axle
with U-bolts. The steering mechanism is
achieved with a king-pin and reverse Elliot
linkage.

This strange name comes from the original
designer of the king-pin type steering
mechanism, a Mr Elliot. He originally
designed the beam axle with bifurcated ends,
with the stub axle carrier fitted into it.
However, his followers quickly discovered that
by changing this round, the assembly was
stronger. So the current practice is reverse
Elliot, i.e. the stub axle carrier fits over the
beam axle (see also the diagram on page 96).

The problem with beam axle suspension is
that, as both wheels are coupled, when one
wheel hits a bump the other is affected. As can
be seen from the diagram, the whole car tips
up when one wheel hits a bump.

Independent suspension

With independent suspension each wheel is
suspended independently of the other. Some
vehicles have independent suspension on all
four wheels, others have it only on the front
wheels. The diagram shows what happens

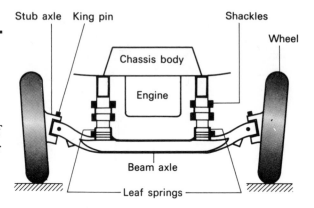

Beam axle suspension

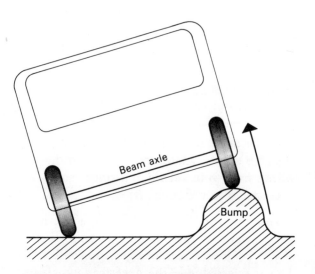

Action of beam axle suspension on bump

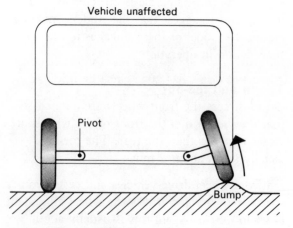

Independent suspension action

when an independently-sprung car hits a
bump. The wheel which hits the bump is
deflected upwards whilst the car remains on an
even keel. This gives better road-holding, even
tyre wear and a more comfortable ride.

Shock absorbers

The purpose of the shock absorber is to
dampen down the spring action and reaction.
Sometimes these are referred to as dampers.
The shock absorber stops the car from
bouncing all over the road each time it hits a
bump. There are two types of shock absorbers:
telescopic and *lever arm*. Each type is identified
by its shape and mounting.

Telescopic shock absorber
The telescopic shock absorber gets its name
from its telescope-like shape and action. The
cylinder is filled with oil or, as it is generally
called, shock absorber fluid. The cylinder is
connected to the axle or suspension with a
mounting eye. The piston and valve assembly,
which are able to move in the cylinder, are
mounted to the vehicle's chassis with the
upper mounting eye or a bolt arrangement.
When the wheel hits a bump the suspension
travels upwards, shortening the distance
between the mounting. Therefore the piston
travels down the cylinder. The resistance of
the oil slows the movement of the piston, so
dampening the shock load on the suspension.
When the wheel has gone over the bump the
suspension rebounds, i.e. the wheel travels
down again and the piston travels up the
cylinder. The resistance of the oil dampens the
suspension movement, so preventing the car
from bouncing along the road.

Lever arm shock absorber
The lever arm shock absorber works in a
similar way to the telescopic shock absorber.

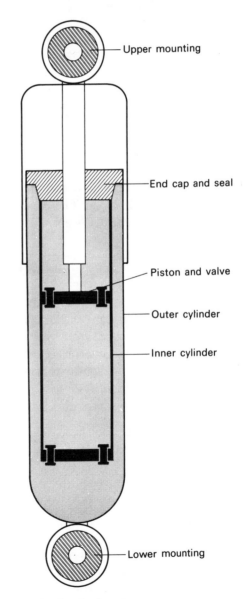

Telescopic shock absorber

The body of the shock absorber is bolted to the vehicle's chassis, with the lever arm attached to the suspension. The suspension movement moves the arm. Inside the shock absorber this arm is attached to a rocker-arm and two pistons in two parallel bores. The pistons move against the resistance of oil in the same way as the telescopic shock absorber. Lever arm shock absorbers usually have provision for being topped up, telescopic ones do not.

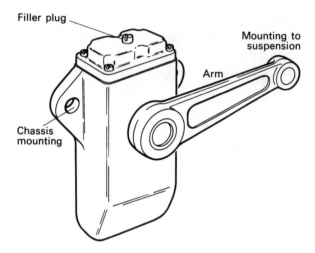

Lever arm shock absorber

Steering linkages

Various layouts of steering linkages are used, depending on the type of vehicle and the system chosen by the designer. The diagram shows the layout of a typical system of linkages.

The steering wheel (1) is situated inside the car; the rest of the components are underneath the front of the car, the steering column (2) connecting them up with the steering wheel by passing through the bulkhead from the underside of the car to the interior. The function of the steering linkages is to convert movement of the steering wheel into movement of the road wheels.

When the steering wheel is turned, this turns the steering column which operates the mechanism in the steering gearbox (3). The cross-shaft (4) is the output from the steering which moves the drop-arm (5). This pushes or pulls the drag link (6) which operates the steering lever (7) which is attached to the offside stub axle (8). The offside wheel is thereby moved in the required direction, about the king pin (9) on the beam axle (10). The track rod (11) is attached to the offside steering

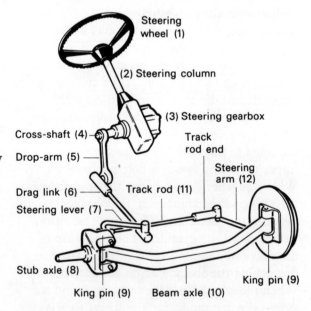

Steering linkages

lever. This moves the steering arm (12) which thereby rotates the nearside stub axle and wheel on its king pin.

One of the main points of wear in the steering system are the ball joints or track-rod ends. To check these for wear, the two components, connected by a ball joint, should be pulled away from each other by hand pressure. A joint in good condition should not have any free play in it at all.

Steering box

The steering box, which is bolted to the chassis, is the main component in the steering linkage. The steering column is attached to the upper part of the steering box. The steering wheel is attached to the top of the steering column. The steering linkages are attached to the lower part of the steering box. The steering box converts movement of the steering wheel, through the column, into movement of the steering linkages. The steering box performs the following tasks:

1 It turns the drive through a right-angle (90 degrees) between the steering wheel and the linkages.
2 It gives a gear ratio of about 14:1. This makes the car easier to drive.
3 It stops bumps from road-surface irregularities being passed onto the driver.

The worm and peg steering box is a very popular type and is used on many types of motor cars and vans. The operation is as follows. The steering column (inner) (1) is turned by the steering wheel (see also the diagram on page 96). This rotates the worm (2) on the ball bearings (8 and 9). As the worm rotates, the peg (3) is moved in the thread of the worm. This moves the rocker shaft (4) which rotates the cross-shaft (5). The cross-shaft (5) is attached to the steering linkage. An adjusting screw is situated on the top-plate (11) to compensate for wear between the peg and the worm. This is usually adjusted every 15 000 km (10 000 miles).

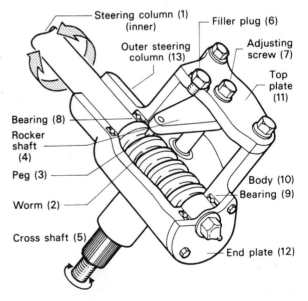

Worm and peg steering box

Rack and pinion

The rack and pinion assembly does the same job as the steering box, but, as can be seen from the diagram, it is a different shape. The rack and pinion is used on many modern light cars as it has the advantages of cheapness and lightness. The rack and pinion is bolted to the chassis or the bulkhead with U-bolts. The steering column connects to the pinion. The arrangement is usually further simplified by connecting the ends of the rack direct to the track-rods ends through a ball joint. The track-rod ends are attached to the steering arms on the hub-carriers.

The pinion is attached to the lower end of the steering column so that it is turned when the steering wheel is moved. The pinion meshes with the rack so that the rack is moved from side to side when the pinion is turned. This, in turn, moves the track-rods to turn the wheels.

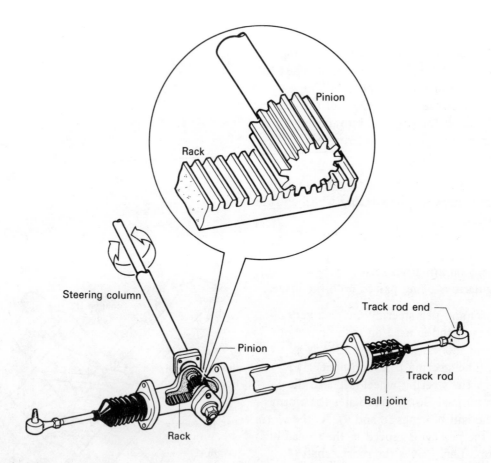

Rack and pinion

Macpherson strut

The Macpherson strut suspension is very popular on cars of all sizes. It is used on many Ford models, Talbots and Peugeots. The strut is a combined suspension swivel and shock absorber. The spring is a coil spring

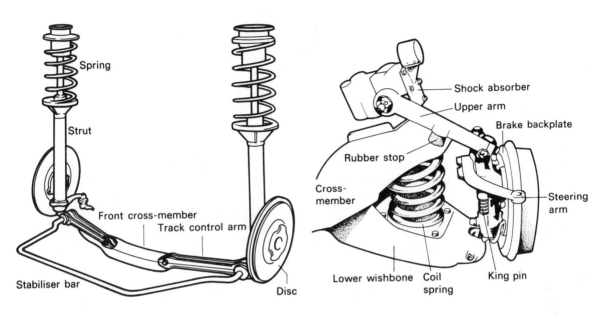

Macpherson strut suspension (as used on Ford cars)

Wishbone suspension (as used on Morris cars)

concentric with the strut. This type of suspension has the advantage of being easy to repair. Generally, a new Macpherson strut is simply fitted complete.

Double wishbone

Double wishbone suspension is so called because the upper and the lower arms of the suspension are shaped like a chicken's wishbone. This type of suspension is used on most Vauxhall models and many other popular cars. The coil spring is concentric with the shock absorber, both fitting inside the wishbones.

Torsion bar

The torsion bar suspension uses a torsion bar spring instead of the more popular coil or leaf spring. This type of suspension is used mainly on light cars, such as the famous Morris Minor, its successor the Morris Marina and the VW Beetle. A lever arm shock absorber is often used as the upper suspension arm.

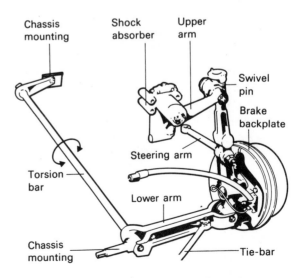

Torsion bar suspension (as used on Morris cars)

Maintenance

Lubrication
The steering joints on most modern cars are pre-packed with grease and sealed for life. However, older cars are fitted with grease nipples so that they can be greased regularly. Some suspension joints use rubber bushes which must be kept free from grease. The steering box is fitted with a filler/level plug. It must be kept filled with gear oil such as 90 SAE up to this level. Where fitted, grease nipples must be lubricated at least every 4500 km (3000 miles) while on older cars 1500 km (1000 mile) intervals are preferable. Steering oil levels should be checked every 7500 km (5000 miles).

Wheel bearings
The front hubs run on two ball- or roller-bearing races. When worn, these make a noise. The wheel bearings should be greased and checked for adjustment every 15 000 km (10 000 miles). Correct adjustment means that the wheels should run free, but have no undue free play when rocked from top to bottom.

Wheel-alignment
The wheel alignment, toe-in or toe-out, should be checked every 15 000 km (10 000 miles). This is done by using optical gauges as shown in the diagram. When the gauges are set up on the wheels the toe-in/toe-out can be read off from the gauge. The track-rod ends are then screwed in or out of the track-rod to give the correct setting.

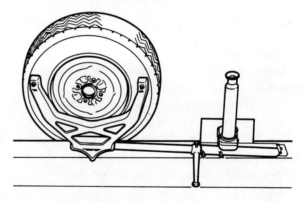

Wheel alignment gauge

Multiple-choice questions

1 The system which protects passengers from road bumps is the:
(a) steering
(b) suspension
(c) braking
(d) transmission

2 The system which guides the car along the chosen path is the:
(a) ignition
(b) braking
(c) suspension
(d) steering

3 *Macpherson strut* and *torsion bar* are types of:
(a) steering
(b) linkages
(c) suspension
(d) steering box

4 '*Toe-in*' and '*toe-out*' relates to the:
(a) front wheels
(b) shock absorbers
(c) rack and pinion
(d) wishbones

5 Even tyre wear is achieved by:
(a) the Ackermann principle
(b) the wishbone
(c) the track rod
(d) the castor angle

6 Self-centering action is achieved by means of:
(a) camber angle
(b) castor angle
(c) king pin inclination
(d) toe-in

7 The inner ends of the wishbones are attached to the chassis; their outer ends are attached to the:
(a) rack and pinion
(b) split pin
(c) drive shaft
(d) king pin

8 One advantage of independent suspension is that:
(a) one wheel can rise independently of the other
(b) both wheels can rise on bumps
(c) bumps are not felt by the passengers
(d) the Ackermann principle is used

9 *Telescopic* and *lever arm* are both types of:
(a) steering rod
(b) steering box
(c) shock absorber
(d) steering wheel

10 Hubs are lubricated with:
(a) wax
(b) water
(c) grease
(d) oil

11 The wheels and tyres

Most cars have four wheels and tyres plus a spare wheel fitted with a tyre provided for emergency use. Should one of the tyres puncture, the car would be immobile if a spare were not provided. To change the punctured wheel for a spare, a jack and wheel-brace are needed. These basic items are provided in most car tool kits.

Some small vehicles have only three road wheels. This gives further economy. With only three wheels on the road wearing out, only three will need replacing at a time. These economy cars are usually very light in weight, less than 425 kg (8 cwt), so they are quite safely supported on three wheels. On the other hand, there are heavy vehicles which need six or more wheels to support their weight.

Functions of wheels and tyres

The functions of the wheels and typres are:

1 To allow the vehicle to roll freely along the road.
2 To support the weight of the vehicle.

3 To act as a first step part of the suspension (see Chapter 10).
4 To transmit to the road surface the
   (a) Driving force,
   (b) Braking force,
   (c) Steering force.

Requirements of wheels and tyres

For the wheels and tyres to be able to carry out their functions efficiently they must be made and maintained to the following basic requirements:

1 They must be perfectly round. If the wheel and tyre are not round then the vehicle will bounce and shake as it goes along the road.
2 They must be stiff, i.e. not able to flex from side to side. A stiff wheel gives precise steering and smooth running.

The laws of most countries require that wheels and tyres fulfil explicit regulations. Details of these regulations are given later in this chapter.

Types of wheels

There are many different types of road wheels in common use. In this chapter we will identify the basic different types and look at their advantages and disadvantages. The main types of wheels are steel-well based, aluminium alloy, wire-spoked, three-piece and two-piece.

Steel-well based wheel

The steel-well based wheel is the most popular type of wheel. This is used on about 90% of all production cars. It is made simply from a centre section which has the outer rim spot welded onto it. It has the advantages of being cheap, light and tough.

Aluminium alloy wheel

This pattern of wheel was originally developed for use on aircraft, the requirements being strength and stiffness coupled with very light weight. The car equivalent fulfils these requirements and has the extra advantage of good looks. The other metal used to alloy with aluminium is magnesium, plus a small amount of silicon. The disadvantages of these alloy wheels, as they are often referred to, are that they are very expensive and very brittle. If the rim is clipped against a kerb or a stone in the road, the wheel might easily be cracked or chipped. This will, of course, quickly deflate the tyre.

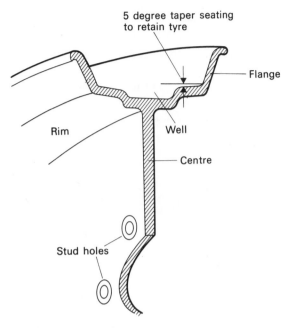

Steel-well based rim

Wire-spoked wheel

The wire-spoked wheel is used only on a small number of sports cars. Unlike the other wheels, which are attached with a ring of studs and nuts, the wire-spoked wheel is usually held onto the hub with a set of splines and a single 'Rudge' nut. The wire-spoked wheel is flexible and therefore slightly springy. It has the advantages of being light, it allows air to pass through to cool the brakes, and it is good-looking. It has the disadvantages of being easily buckled, especially if the spokes become loose.

Wire-spoke wheel construction

Three-piece wheel

Illustrated is a three-piece wheel as used on most HGVs and PSVs. The components of this wheel are made from medium-carbon steel, which is much harder and stronger than the low-carbon steel used for pressed car wheels. The three pieces of this wheel are the main wheel, the detachable side and the retaining spring ring. This detachable construction is used so that the tyre can be removed and refitted easily.

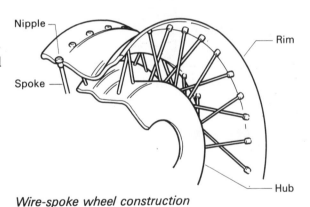

Three-piece steel wheel

Two-piece wheel

A two-piece wheel is made from two symmetrical wheel-halves which are bolted together with a ring of nuts and bolts. This construction is designed to give easy removal and refitting of the tyre. The two-piece wheel is used on small-diameter wheels such as those on scooters and specialised vehicles.

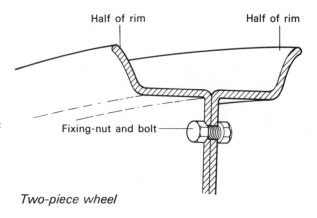

Two-piece wheel

Tyres

The basic construction of all vehicle tyres is very similar, and the diagram shows the names used to describe the many parts of the tyre. The wire bead forms the shape of the tyre, with the rubber and textile parts running from one bead to the other. The two main types of tyres are the cross-ply tyre and the radial-ply tyre.

Cross-ply tyre

As can be seen in the diagram, the plies run across each other, all at about 45 degrees to the bead. Hence the name 'cross-ply'.

Radial-ply tyre

The radial-ply tyre is becoming more commonly used than the cross-ply tyre.

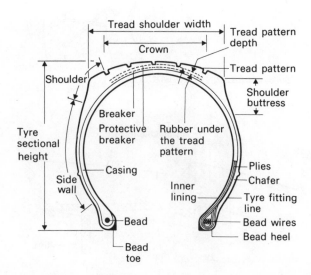

Parts of the tyre

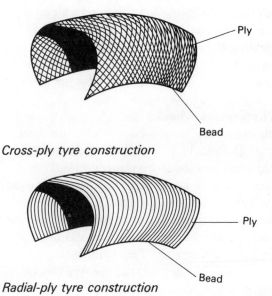

Cross-ply tyre construction

Radial-ply tyre construction

Radial tyre tread for bad weather conditions

Radial tyre tread for high speeds

Generally, radial ply tyres roll more freely, giving more miles per gallon and longer tread-life than cross-plies. The plies of the radial-ply tyre run, as their name implies, radially, i.e. at right-angles to the bead.

Tyre treads
Different types of tyre treads are used by different manufacturers. Examples are shown in the diagrams. The reason for the use of different tread patterns is the varying uses to which the vehicle may be put. For instance, whether the car is to be driven slowly about town, fast on motorways or is for offroad use, like Land Rovers and other farm vehicles.

Water is ejected sideways so that the tyre maintains contact with the road surface

Inner tube
This consists of a rubber tube and valve, which is used to retain the air inside the tyre. A rim tape is needed to prevent spokes puncturing the inner tube when fitted to wire wheels.

Tubeless tyre
Most modern cars use tubeless tyres, i.e. they do not have inner tubes. The tyre forms an airtight seal against the wheel rim.

Valve
To hold the air in the inner tube or tubeless tyre a valve is fitted. When air is pumped into

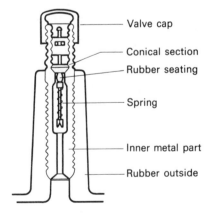

Schrader valve

Valve cap

Conical section

Rubber seating

Spring

Inner metal part

Rubber outside

the tyre the valve core is forced downwards to allow the air to pass. When the air-intake stops, the pressure of the air in the tyre helps to keep the valve closed.

Tyre sizes

The size of the tyre depends on the size of the wheel. The diagram shows how a wheel is measured, the important sizes being the diameter and the width. The tyre is measured as shown. The diameter of the tyre is always given in inches. The width of cross-ply tyres is given in inches, that of radials in millimetres. For example:

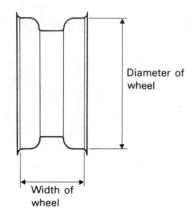

Wheel sizes

Width	×	*Diameter*
5.20	×	13 cross-ply
145	×	13 radial-ply.

Tyre regulations

The laws on tyre fitting and usage in the UK and most European countries can be summarised as follows:

1 Radial or cross-ply tyres can be fitted to all vehicles.
2 If only two radial-ply tyres are fitted, these must be fitted on the rear wheels.
3 Cross-ply and radial-ply tyres must *not* be mixed on the same axle.
4 The tyre pressure must be kept within the manufacturer's settings.
5 The tread must not be less than 1 mm deep for the entire circumference over 75% of the tread-width.
6 The tread and side-walls must be free from large cuts, abrasions or bubbles.

Wheel-rotation

To give even tyre-wear over all the vehicle's tyres, including the spare, the wheels and tyres are moved around. The diagram shows a typical system of wheel-rotation which is suitable for vehicles which are fitted with identical wheels and tyres.

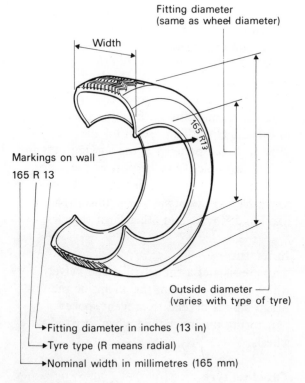

Tyre sizes

The system of rotation can be summarised as follows:

Nearside front (N/S/F) to nearside rear (N/S/R)
Offside front (O/S/F) to offside rear (O/S/R)
Nearside rear (N/S/R) to offside front (O/S/F)
Offside rear (O/S/R) to spare
Spare to nearside front (N/S/F)

Jacking up to change a wheel

When jacking the car up a firm place under the chassis or axle should be chosen. To prevent the vehicle from rolling away when it is being jacked up a chock should be placed behind the wheels which remain on the ground.

Tyre-changing

The diagrams show the sequence followed when changing a tyre on a wheel:

1   A key is used to unscrew the valve and so deflate the tyre.
2   The tyre bead is pressed away from the wheel-rim edge on both sides of the tyre.
3   One side of the tyre is levered off the wheel.

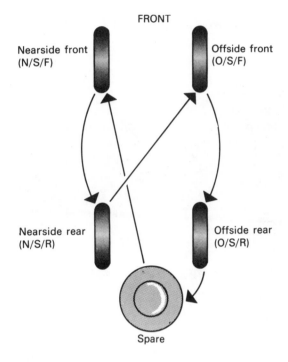

Wheel- and tyre-rotation

4   The other side of the tyre is levered off, thus removing the tyre from the wheel.
The procedure is reversed for refitting.

Removal of a tyre: a key is used to unscrew the valve and deflate the tyre

Removal of a tyre: the bead is pressed away from the rim edge on both sides of the tyre

Removal of a tyre: one side is levered off

Removal of a tyre: the other side is levered off

When inflating three-piece wheels there is a danger of the components coming apart if they are not properly seated. A safety cage should be used, behind which the tyre must be inflated to prevent possible injury to the person doing the job.

Multiple-choice questions

1 The requirements of a wheel are that they must be:
   (a) round and stiff
   (b) round and flat
   (c) stiff and solid
   (d) round and wide

2 An advantage of aluminium wheels is that they are:
   (a) brittle
   (b) tough
   (c) wide
   (d) light

3 If only two radial ply tyres are fitted, they must be fitted to:
   (a) both front wheels
   (b) both rear wheels
   (c) opposite corners
   (d) the near side

4 The minimum legal tread depth is:
   (a) 5 mm
   (b) 10 mm
   (c) 1 mm
   (d) 3 mm

5 One disadvantage of wire wheels is that:
   (a) an inner tube is needed
   (b) they are too narrow
   (c) they look ugly
   (d) special tyres are needed

6 The figures 165×13 on radial ply tyres refer to:
   (a) width and pressure
   (b) width and diameter
   (c) diameter and pressure
   (d) type and make

7 What safety precaution should be taken
when inflating the tyres on a three-piece
wheel for a HGV:
(a) always use a gauge
(b) never clean them
(c) never use a gauge
(d) always use a cage

8 *Tread, bead* and *wall* are all parts of a:
(a) tube
(b) tyre
(c) rim
(d) wheel

9 The position of road wheels is often
changed to:
(a) give even tyre wear
(b) slow down the tyre wear
(c) give smooth steering
(d) give better traction

10 Two-piece wheels are found on:
(a) hatchback cars
(b) light vans
(c) scooters
(d) PSVs

12 The braking system

All vehicles must be fitted with some form of braking system. The system can operate on a set of rods and cables, called *mechanical brakes*, or it can use fluids in pipes, called *hydraulic brakes*. The law in all countries requires that vehicles have at least two independent braking systems fitted. These are normally a foot-brake and a hand-brake, so called because they are operated by foot and hand, respectively.

Function

The braking system does more than just stop the car, it should:

1 Stop the vehicle, i.e. bring the vehicle to a halt from whatever speed it is travelling at.
2 Slow the vehicle, i.e. be capable of reducing the speed from, say, 50 kph (30 mph) to 25 kph (15 mph).
3 Provide a parking brake, to hold the vehicle firmly on either level ground or on an incline.

Brake regulations

The law in all countries requires braking systems to meet a legal minimum of regulations and to meet a certain set of standards. Basically these requirements are as follows:

1 The vehicle must be fitted with two independent braking systems. This is usually achieved by having the main braking system operated by the foot on all four wheels, with the hand-brake operating on the rear wheels only. The hand-brake forms the parking brake and the emergency brake should the main braking system fail.
2 The main foot brake system must be capable of giving deceleration of at least 50%.
3 The emergency hand-brake must be capable of giving deceleration equal to at least 25%.

Deceleration means the opposite of acceleration. The terms used in (2) and (3) are those used when measuring the rate of deceleration. Deceleration is measured on a powered brake tester. The reading is given so that it can be read straight from the meter dial, as on a Tapley meter, or a rolling road tester.

Mechanical brakes

Early cars were fitted with mechanical brakes, both the foot-brake pedal and the hand-brake lever being connected to the brake drums by a series of rods and cables. Current vehicles use mechanical linkages only for their hand-brake mechanism. However, mechanical linkages are commonly used on trailers, motor cycles and specialist vehicles like works trucks. An operating cam, as used on a motor cycle, is shown. The pull on the cable twists the cam to apply the brake shoes against the drum.

Mechanical linkages have a few disadvantages: for example, the cables stretch, which involves frequent adjustment of the mechanism and eventual cable-replacement. The rods are soon bent if caught on twigs or stones on the road. This can lead to uneven braking. The yokes and Clevis pins wear, so causing free play which again must be removed by adjustment. The greatest disadvantage, as far as the mechanic is concerned, is that each rod and cable has to be adjusted to give even braking

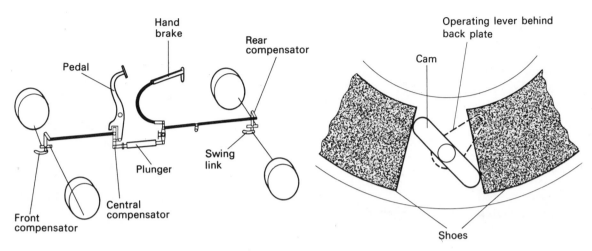

Mechanical brake layout (cable)   *Operating cam on mechanical brakes*

on all the road wheels. This can only be done by trial and error methods tested on the road. Therefore brake-adjusting on these mechanical systems is a time-consuming and trying job.

Hydraulic brakes

With hydraulic brakes the transmission of force from the brake pedal to the brake shoes is through hydraulic fluid. The system works on the principle that as the brake fluid is a liquid it cannot be compressed, and that any pressure applied to a fluid in one direction is transmitted equally in all directions. This principle is called Pascal's Law. Pascal was a French scientist who lived between 1623 and 1662. He also gave his name to the unit used to measure pressure, for instance in brake pipes. This is the kilopascal (kPa) (for conversion, approximately 100 kPa equals 15 psi).

A typical hydraulic braking system is shown in the diagram. As can be seen, the main components of the hydraulic brake system are the master cylinder, the slave cylinders at each wheel (or wheel cylinders, as they are called), the shoe assemblies and the pipes which interconnect the cylinder and transmit the pressure through the fluid.

Before looking at each component of the braking system in turn the student should have an overview of the basic hydraulic system used on current motor cars and light commercial vehicles. The layout is usually such that the master cylinder is attached to the front bulkhead so that it can be operated by the driver's right foot. Each wheel has its own brake assembly. Generally, this is either drum

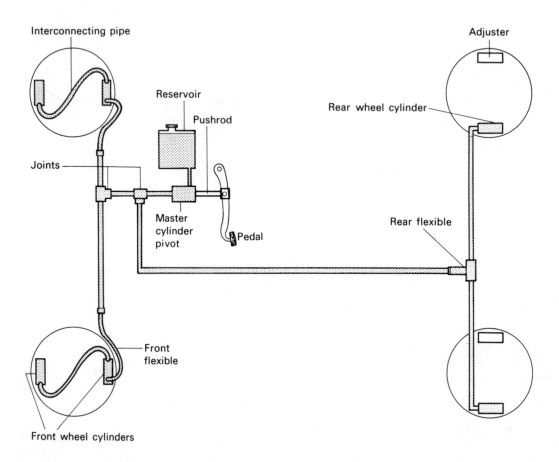

Layout of hydraulic brakes

brakes on all four wheels, or drum brakes on the rear wheels and disc brakes on the front wheels. When the driver's right foot is pressed on the brake pedal the pedal pushes the pushrod, so actuating the master cylinder. The master cylinder sends fluid under pressure along the brake pipes to each wheel cylinder. The wheel cylinders operate the brake shoes against drums to slow or stop the car. With disc brake systems the equivalent of the wheel cylinder is the caliper, which forces the pad against the disc.

Transmission of force by fluid

The operation of the hydraulic system can be modelled with a tube fitted with a piston at

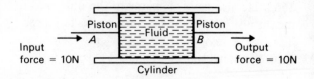

Equal-size pistons in a cylinder

each end as in the diagram. Between the two pistons is a fluid. If you want to do this experiment in class, water is the best fluid to use as it makes the least mess if spilt on the desk or floor. Push one piston into the tube with one thumb whilst feeling with the other thumb the force that the other piston exerts outwards. Thumb pressure will tell you that both forces are equal. If you wish, you could, of course, measure the forces by using spring-scales.

The pressure exerted on the fluid is dependent on the cross-sectional area of the piston. In the above experiment the pistons are of equal area as they both fit into the same size tube. Pressure can be found by the formula

$$\text{Pressure} = \frac{\text{Force}}{\text{Cross-sectional area}}$$

In the SI system the unit of pressure is the pascal (Pa), but for practical use in motor vehicles the kilopascal (kPa) is used, i.e. 1000 pascals. This is found by dividing the force in newtons (N) by the area in square metres (m²) × 1000:

$$\text{kPa} = \frac{\text{N}}{1\ \text{m}^2} \times 1000$$

i.e. 1 kPa = 1000 N spread over an area of 1 square metre.

The diagram shows two pistons, each of different sizes, interconnected by a tube. It demonstrates how the force is changed with the difference in cross-sectional areas. Piston *B* is twice the area of piston *A*, so the force on piston *B* is twice as great.

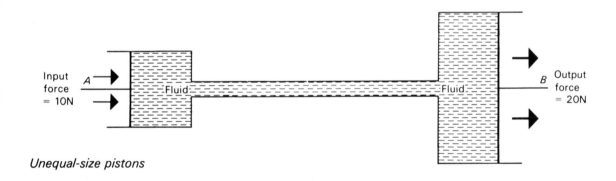

Unequal-size pistons

Master cylinder

The master cylinder is bolted to the bulkhead just in front of the driver. The pedal is connected to the lower end of the master cylinder and the outlet pipe to the wheel cylinder is connected to the upper part. The fluid reservoir is placed to one side.

Operation of master cylinder
The internal parts of the master cylinder are shown in the diagram. When the pedal is depressed it acts on the master cylinder pushrod. The pushrod pushes up the cylinder bore against the light resistance of the spring.

As the piston travels up the cylinder, the cup washer seal closes off the passage between the fluid reservoir and the cylinder. This prevents fluid leaving the cylinder through that passage. Instead, it is pushed upwards and out through the check valve into the hydraulic pipes. The fluid is not pumped or pressurised but displaced under pressure. Movement of the fluid in the cylinder pushes up the rest of the fluid. The fluid at the far end operates the wheel cylinders (to be discussed later). When the driver's foot is taken off the brake pedal the spring returns the piston and the pushrod back to where they were, i.e. the bottom end of their travel. Therefore the pressure is taken off the brake fluid. The springs on the brake shoes return the displaced fluid from the wheel cylinders along the brake pipes back to the master cylinder. Any loss of fluid in the system is topped up by the reservoir.

Brake master cylinders are sometimes mounted horizontally, and on some vehicles they are under the floor rather than on the bulkhead.

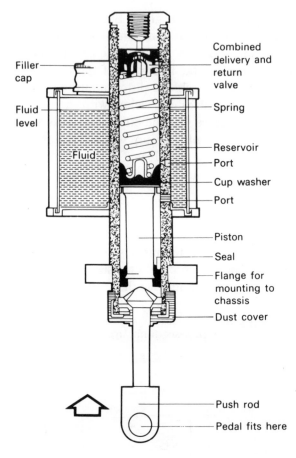

Construction of brake master cylinder

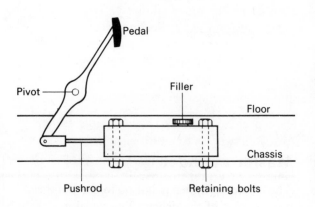

Underfloor master cylinder

Wheel cylinders

The wheel cylinders are attached to the brake back-plates and operate the brake shoes against the brake drum. Wheel cylinders are sometimes referred to as *slave cylinders*, being subordinate to the master cylinder.

Fluid enters the wheel cylinder from the brake pipe, being displaced into the wheel cylinder by the action of the master cylinder. The further the brake pedal is depressed the more is displaced and the greater the amount of fluid entering the wheel cylinder. The diagram shows the cross-section of a wheel cylinder. As can be seen, it is an outer cylinder fitted with a piston. A rubber seal fits into the groove around the piston to give a fluid-tight seal between the piston and the cylinder walls. As the brake fluid is forced into the wheel cylinder the piston is forced outwards by the fluid. Illustrated is the wheel cylinder in the contracted and expanded positions. The expansion is caused by the fluid filling the cylinder.

The amount of travel that the wheel cylinder is allowed is controlled by the wear on the brake linings and the amount of adjustment taken up by the brake adjusters. The wheel cylinder is returned to the contracted position by the springs fitted to the brake shoes. When the brake pedal is returned to the top the springs force back the wheel cylinders and the fluid is returned to the master cylinder.

The wheel cylinder may have one piston, as already shown, or two pistons as shown in the diagrams. The single cylinder is used on twin leading shoe arrangements, the double on leading and trailing shoe arrangements.

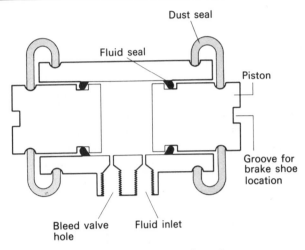

Brake wheel cylinder (double piston)

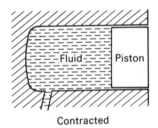

Wheel cylinder (single piston): contracted

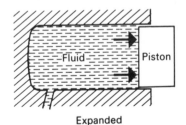

Wheel cylinder (single piston): expanded

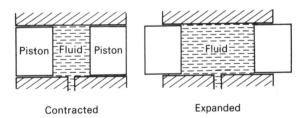

Brake wheel cylinder (double piston)

Brake pipes

There are two classifications of brake pipes: *metal non-flexible* pipes and *rubber flexible* pipes. Both types are capable of withstanding the same very high pressures from the fluid inside. In fact, both types of pipes, when new, can withstand pressures several times higher than those likely to be encountered under normal braking. This is to give a *factor of safety* to the system, so allowing for extreme conditions and the deterioration of materials.

Metal brake pipe with flared end and connector

Metal non-flexible pipes

The metal pipes, which are made from varying mixtures of iron, copper and nickel, are liable to corrosion. When rust sets in the metal is dangerously weakened. In this case the pipes must be replaced by new ones.

Metal pipes must be firmly attached to the body or chassis to prevent flexing. Bending or flexing of the metal can quickly lead to failure and hence the loss of brakes.

Rubber flexible pipes

Rubber flexible pipes, or hoses, are used in places where flexibility of the brake pipe is necessary. Normally three or four short flexible hoses are used on each car. They are positioned to allow the wheels to rise and fall with the suspension. The rubber hoses are reinforced with metal strands on the inside to enable the hose to withstand the high pressure and with a coil of wire around the outside to prevent chafing should it touch the bodywork.

Flexible rubber hose attached to a metal pipe

The brake pipes are connected together with screw joints. Inside the screw joints curved surfaces are used. When the joint is tightened these surfaces are held against each other to prevent fluid-leakage. The ends of the flexible hoses are ready-shaped, the flexible hoses

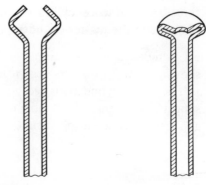

Single flare on metal brake pipes   *Double flare on metal brake pipes*

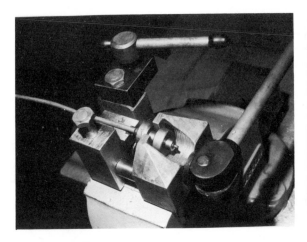

Brake-pipe flaring tool. (a) pipe installed in bottom die; (b) top die in place ready to make flared end

being bought complete with ends. The metal pipe is bought in rolls and cut to length as required. The ends of the metal pipe can take the form of a single flare or a double flare. Both types of ends are put onto the metal pipe using a brake-pipe flaring tool.

When making up a brake pipe it is essential that the instructions for the particular machine are closely followed, and that the correct flare is used. Often brake pipes have different flares at each end. In this case care must be taken to fit the pipe the correct way round.

Brake shoes

A brake shoe is shown in the diagram. These are used on drum brakes, two to each wheel. Also shown is the cross-section of a brake shoe. The shoe itself is metal fitted with an asbestos lining. The lining may be riveted or bonded to the metal shoe. In the bonding process heat is used to stick the resin and asbestos lining to the shoe. The grooves in the shoe ends are to enable and ensure its correct locations against the wheel cylinders and adjusters. The holes are for the attachment of return springs.

Asbestos is used as a lining material for contact with the brake drum because it offers a high coefficient of friction, is resistant to burning and will not weld itself to the brake

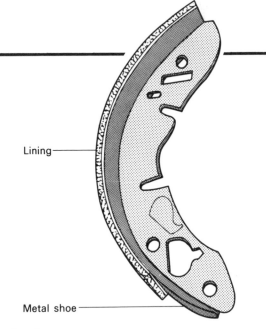

Lining

Metal shoe

Brake shoe

drum. The dust from the asbestos used for brake linings is dangerous. Care must be taken to avoid breathing in this dust, or any other fine dust, as this can cause lung cancer.

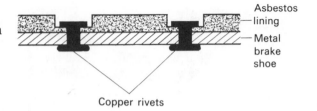

Cross-section of brake shoe

Brake shoe layouts

There are two main types of drum layout for brakes:

1 Leading and trailing shoe layout
2 Twin leading shoe layout

The leading edge of the shoe is the edge of the shoe which comes into contact with the drum as it rotates. On leading shoe arrangements the leading edge tends to bite into the drum and apply the brakes harder. The leading edge therefore tends to wear first.

Twin leading shoe brakes are usually fitted to the front wheel of cars as they give the greatest braking effort for their size. However, when the car is being reversed the twin leading shoe brakes become twin trailing shoe brakes. These are very inefficient, and are therefore not very good at stopping the car.

As can be seen in the diagram, there are two wheel cylinders, one to operate each brake shoe. When the fluid pressure moves the wheel cylinder's piston, the shoe is forced against the drum at its leading edge. The back of each wheel cylinder is used as a pivot for the opposite shoe. The springs serve to return the shoes when the pressure is released.

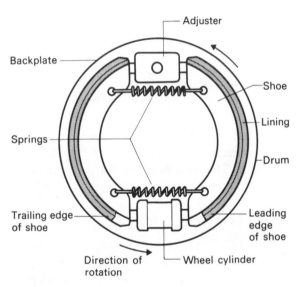

Brake-shoe arrangement (leading and trailing)

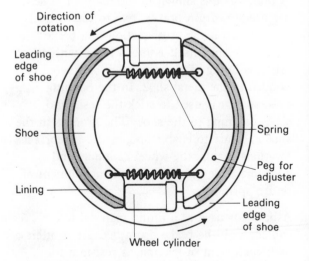

Brake-shoe arrangement (twin leading shoe)

Brake-adjusters

A taper wedge brake-adjuster is shown. This type of adjuster is used on most leading and trailing shoe arrangements. Also shown is the adjuster cross-section contracted and the adjuster expanded to take up the brakes. A squared-end spanner, usually 3 mm ($\frac{1}{8}$ inch), is used to turn the taper wedge. As the screw goes into the brake-adjuster the tapered end forces out the wedges. The wedges press against the ends of the shoes, so taking up the free play.

Another type of adjuster is the snail cam. This is usually made integral with the brake back plate, whereas the taper wedge type is generally only screwed to the brake back plate. The snail cam is so called because it is the same shape as a snail shell.

The adjuster is shown in the off position and fully adjusted. This type of adjuster is used on most twin leading shoe arrangements. Like the taper wedge, adjustment is made by turning the spindle end with a square tool. From 'off' to the fully adjusted position is achieved by turning the spindle, and hence the spiral cam, less than one turn. The taper wedge requires many turns to adjust it. Hence the taper wedge gives finer adjustment.

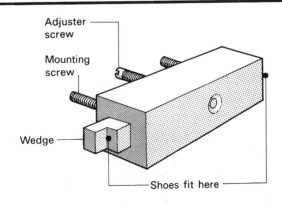

Taper wedge brake-adjuster

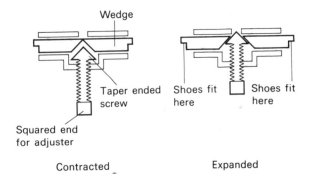

Taper wedge brake-adjuster: contracted and expanded

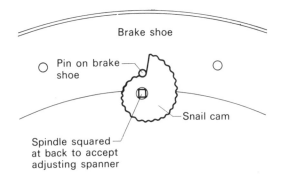

Snail cam adjuster in 'off' position

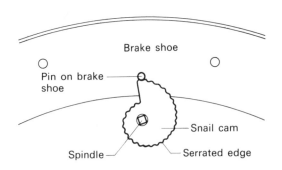

Snail cam adjuster in 'on' fully adjusted position

Hand brake

The hand brake operates the brakes on the rear wheels. It consists of a hand lever near the driver connected by a cable or rod to a mechanism in the brake drums alongside the wheel cylinder. Sometimes this is incorporated in the wheel cylinder. The diagram shows a hand brake arrangement using a swivel-tree compensator. The lever pulls the main cable which, in turn, pulls the two side cables. These activate the mechanism on the back plate to apply the brakes. The swivel-tree compensator changes the direction of pull of the cable and increases the leverage by the difference in the length of its arms. The problem with the swivel tree is that, when subjected to water and mud, they quickly seize up. Also shown is an alternative arrangement. In this, just two cables are used, compensation for adjustment being taken up by the rear cable being able to slide.

To allow for cable stretch and wear in the joints a screw adjustment is fitted. This is a screw and nut arrangement fitted through a yoke. The nut is screwed along the threaded end until the slack is removed, then it is secured with the lock-nut.

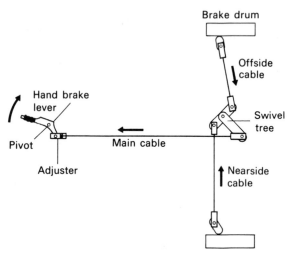

Hand-brake layout (swivel tree)

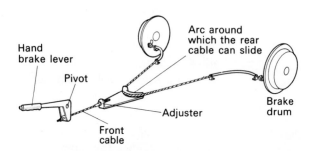

Hand-brake layout (two-cable type)

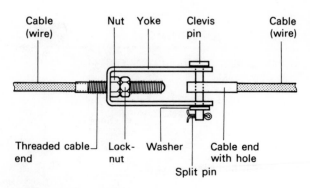

Hand-brake adjuster

Disc brakes

Disc brakes have several advantages over drum brakes, namely:

1   Less likely to 'fade' (reduction in braking efficiency through an increase in temperature of the friction surfaces after several brake applications).
2   Open to the air, and therefore kept cooler.
3   Easy to change friction surfaces, i.e. pads can be changed without stripping.
4   Give greater braking effort for size and weight with the aid of a brake servo.
5   Self-adjusting.

Disc brakes are used on the front of many cars. Although they were originally made for racing cars they quickly found their way onto ordinary saloon cars.

The diagram shows the cross-section of a disc brake arrangement. Its operation is similar to that of the wheel cylinders in drum brakes. Fluid enters the caliper and forces the pistons out. The pistons push the pads against the disc so giving the braking effort. The pad is made from a compound of asbestos, resin and various metals on a metal back plate — similar to a brake shoe.

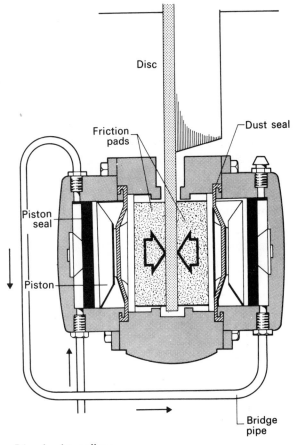

Disc brake caliper

Brake-adjustment

Brake-adjustment should be carried out every 7500 km (5000 miles) to compensate for wear of the friction surfaces. With the car jacked up, the adjusting screw should be turned until the wheel can no longer be turned by hand. The adjuster should then be backed off until the wheel rotates freely. This technique does require a little practice until the ideal setting can be judged. Disc brakes are self-adjusting, but when adjusting brakes it is wise to check that the disc brakes are in good condition and operating properly.

When the wheel-adjusters have been seen to, the hand cable can be taken up if necessary. The lever should pull up between about three and five notches or 'clicks'. However, this can vary from car to car.

Brake bleeding

To get air out of the hydraulic system it must be bled, i.e. the fluid must be pumped out until all the air is expelled with it. This is necessary after fitting new components to the hydraulic system.

Set up the rubber tube and jar as in the diagram. Open the bleed valve by unscrewing half a turn or so and press the pedal to force out the fluid and air. Keep the master cylinder topped up with new fluid as you do this. After four or five presses on the pedal, hold the pedal down and tighten up the bleed valve. Two people are needed to do this on most cars.

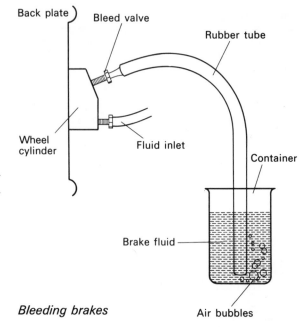

Bleeding brakes

Multiple-choice questions

1 Deceleration is measured using a:
   (a) dynometer
   (b) Tapley meter
   (c) steep hill
   (d) dwell meter

2 Disc brake pad linings are made from:
   (a) iron
   (b) brass
   (c) asbestos
   (d) steel

3 *Snail cam* and *taper wedge* are types of:
   (a) disc brake
   (b) drum brake
   (c) master cylinder
   (d) brake adjuster

4 Hydraulic brake systems are bled to:
   (a) remove air
   (b) let in air
   (c) remove fluid
   (d) top-up the fluid

5 The leading edge of a brake shoe is the one which:
   (a) touches the drum last
   (b) is used on disc brakes
   (c) touches the drum first
   (d) is used on hand brakes

6 The slave cylinder is expanded by:
   (a) brake fluid
   (b) air pressure
   (c) a spring
   (d) rubber seals

7 Double flare and single flare are types of:
   (a) nipple
   (b) hand brake cable
   (c) brake pipe end
   (d) brake fluid

8 Disc brakes are:
   (a) more likely to fade than drum brakes
   (b) less likely to fade than drum brakes
   (c) in constant need of adjustment
   (d) only fitted to sports cars

9 Hand brake adjustment is provided to:
   (a) allow for cable stretch
   (b) allow for lining wear
   (c) allow for wear in the lever
   (d) allow for bleeding.

10 The efficiency of the foot brake must be at least:
   (a) 25%
   (b) 50%
   (c) 100%
   (d) 75%

13 The electrical system

The electrical system is made up of several separate circuits or independent systems. Each circuit with its components does a separate job. The electrical items are spread across the length and breadth of the car, in some cases serving to operate or control the mechanical components.

The diagram shows the main components of the electrical system as they are laid out in a typical car. The wiring is connected in a 'loom,' i.e. each wire is bound up, where possible, with several others. A cloth or plastic coating is used to cover the loom.

Each of the electrical components will be described in full, but first let us look at all of them briefly before studying the details. The front sidelamps and the tail-lamps are to show the other drivers that there is a car on the road. The headlamps show the driver where he is going and the stop-lamps warn following drivers that he is about to slow down or stop. The battery is the reservoir of electrical current which is kept topped up by the alternator (or dynamo). The starter motor spins the engine over to start it. The horn is used to warn other road-users of the car's presence in an emergency. The gauges keep the driver aware of the vehicle's condition, and the switches operate the various components.

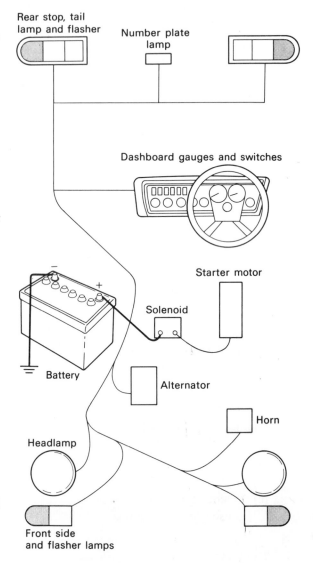

Layout of electrical components

Battery

The battery forms the central energy store of the electrical system. All the vehicle's electrical components are either directly or indirectly connected to the battery. This leads to the rule which must be carried out when working on any electrical component or section of wiring:

Before carrying out any electrical work always disconnect the battery.

The battery is made up of pairs of electrolytic plates fitted into a case which is filled with electrolyte. The plates are *positive* and *negative*.

The positive plates are made from a lead grid filled with lead peroxide; the negative plates are grids filled with spongey lead. In each cell, i.e. division of the case, the plates are grouped to form a *cell-pack*. The plates are put together in the form of a large sandwich in the order of negative, positive, negative, etc. The number of plates is always odd. A negative plate is used at each end and plastic separators keep the plates apart. All the positive plates in each cell are connected together, as are the negative plates. The cell plates are then connected positive to negative across the top of the battery. This leaves a positive terminal at one end and a negative at the other.

Each cell in a battery gives 2V; so a 12V battery has 6 cells and a 6V battery has 3 cells.

The battery case can be made from either hard rubber or one of the many plastic materials. The case must be:

1 Rigid to hold the plates in position.
2 Tough to resist bangs and abrasions.
3 Able to withstand very low and high temperatures.
4 Able to withstand the corrosive action of the electrolyte.

Electrolyte

Electrolyte is a mixture of sulphuric acid and distilled water. Sulphuric acid is also known by its chemical formula, H_2SO_4. Distilled water is water which has been evaporated and condensed to rid it of impurities. Sulphuric acid should be treated with care, because, if spilt, it can cause skin burns.

Hydrometer

The state of charge of the battery can be tested by using a hydrometer. This comprises a glass tube with a rubber bulb at the top end and a flexible rubber tube at the bottom end. Inside

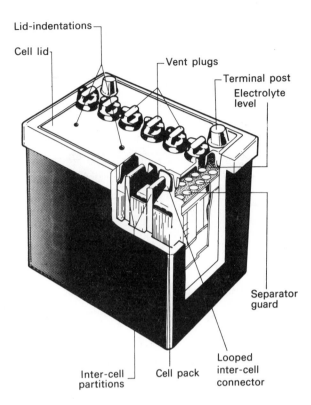

Battery

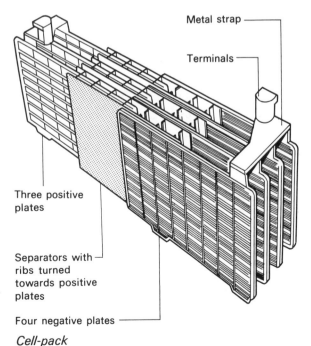

Cell-pack

the tube is a plastic float. Electrolyte from each cell in turn is drawn into the hydrometer by squeezing the rubber bulb and releasing it to suck up the liquid. The state of charge is determined by reading from the float at the electrolyte level.

The float is marked as in the diagram, i.e. with sections for fully charged, half-charged and dead flat. Sometimes these are simply different colours — green, yellow and red, respectively. The numbers indicate the relative density (RD) of the liquid, as shown in the table.

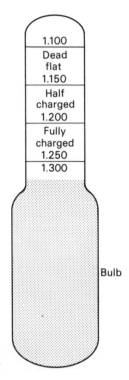

Hydrometer float

Colour	Number	State of charge	Float Position
Green	1.300	Fully charged	Float high in electrolyte
Yellow	1.200	Half-charged	Float mid-height in electrolyte
Red	1.100	Dead flat	Float sunk into electrolyte

Battery maintenance

Being situated under the bonnet the battery gets warm. Also its own action heats up the electrolyte, which causes a loss of liquid. This must be replenished by topping up with distilled water. The level of the electrolyte should be kept 2 mm above the tops of the plates or the plate protectors. The electrolyte level must be checked regularly, at least once a month.

Dynamo

The dynamo is situated along the side of the engine. It is driven by the fan belt from the crankshaft pulley. The dynamo generates electricity for the following uses:

1   To power the electrical components when the engine is running (for example, the lights and the windscreen-wipers).

2   To keep the battery fully charged so that current is available to operate the electrical starter and the parking lights.

The dynamo is attached to the engine with three bolts. Two are along one side of the casing, the other is on the opposite side. This single bolt is mounted on an elongated bracket

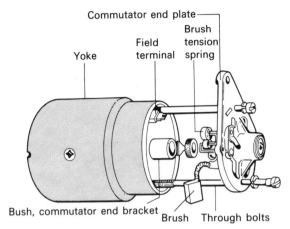

Construction of dynamo

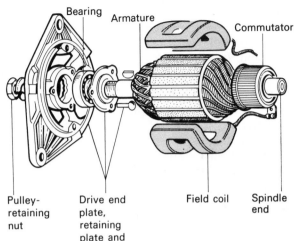

to enable the fan belt to be adjusted. (This is discussed further in the section on the cooling system, page 56.)

The main components of the dynamo are shown in the diagram. These are the casing, the armature, the commutator, the end plates, the pulley and the fan.

Regulation
To control the rate of charge from the dynamo to the battery a regulator is fitted. This controls the amperage of the charge to the battery, depending on the state of charge of the battery. The regulator also controls the voltage from the dynamo to the battery, and it switches on and off the current between the dynamo and the battery, depending on the battery's state of charge and the dynamo's output.

Charging circuit
The wiring diagram of the charging circuit is shown. The red warning light on the dashboard comes on when the dynamo is not charging (usually at idling speeds). If the light comes on at speeds above tick-over or when the ignition is switched off, this indicates a fault in the wiring or one of the components.

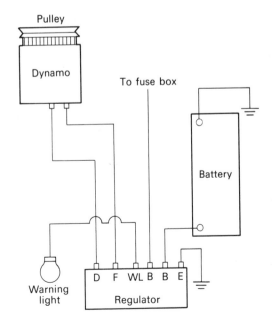

Charging circuit. D = dynamo; F = field; WL = warning light; B = battery; E = earth

Alternator

An alternator is fitted as one alternative to the dynamo. Its purpose is the same as those of the dynamo, i.e. to power the electrical components and keep the battery topped up. The alternator has the following advantages over the dynamo for equal power outputs:

1 It is smaller — the alternator is about half the size of the dynamo.
2 It is lighter.
3 The alternator still charges at engine idling speeds.

The components of the alternator are shown in the diagram. The two main components are the rotor and the stator. Slip rings and brushes are used in the alternator in place of the commutator and brushes, which are used in the dynamo.

Alternator

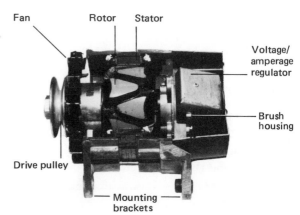

Alternator cut away to show components

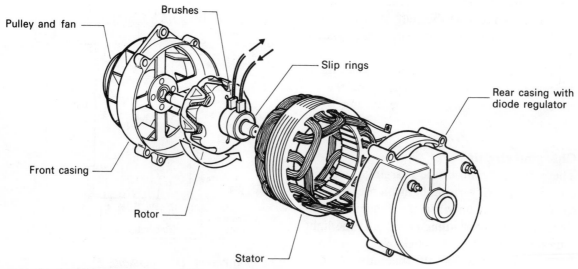

The components of the alternator

Alternator circuit

The diagram for an alternator circuit is shown. The warning light comes on when the alternator is not charging. The regulator is built into the alternator, electrically controlling the voltage and the current going to the battery. Because the regulator is incorporated into the alternator the engine must not be run with the wiring disconnected. If this were done, the alternator regulator might be damaged.

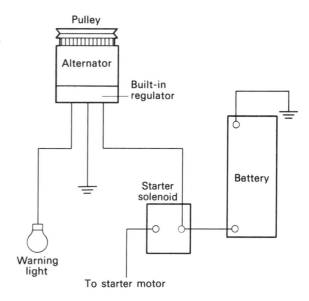

Alternator wiring diagram

Starter motor

The function of the starter motor is to turn the engine over fast enough to initiate combustion. It does this by converting electrical energy into mechanical energy. The starter motor is bolted to the lower rear part of the engine. The main parts of the starter are shown. These are the casing, the armature, the end plates and the driving pinion. The internal construction of the starter is very similar to that of the dynamo.

The teeth of the driving pinion of the starter motor are engaged automatically with those on the flywheel ring gear when the starter motor is switched on. As very heavy cable is needed to transmit the high amperage current from

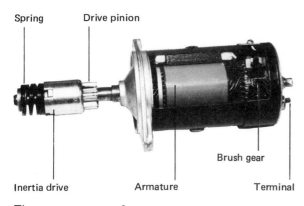

The components of a starter motor

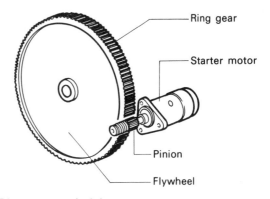

Ring gear and pinion

the battery to the starter motor, a solenoid method of switching is used. The dashboard switch operates the solenoid, and the solenoid switches the high amperage current to the starter motor. In other words, the solenoid is a remote-controlled high-amperage switch.

Starter circuit

The starter circuit is shown in the diagram. The solenoid is situated on either the bulkhead or the inner wing. In either case it is near the battery or the starter motor, so that the minimum amount of heavy starter cable type wire is needed.

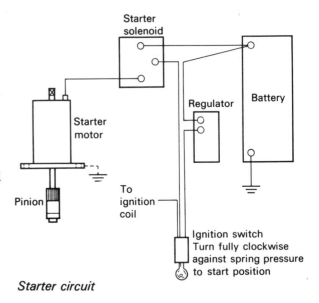

Starter circuit

Light and warning systems

Horn

The horn is fitted as a warning device to other road-users. It is positioned somewhere at the front of the car, just behind the radiator grille. The horn is operated by a horn-push or ring on the steering wheel or column. This is situated so that it is very easily reached by the driver's hand.

Horn wiring

The horn wiring diagram shows how the horn-push is wired in the earth-return to reduce the amount of cable to the minimum.

Side-lights

The law in all countries requires vehicles to be fitted with lights which will illuminate the vehicle so that it can be seen after sunset or during bad weather conditions such as fog or storms. The most usual convention is white lights to the front and red lights to the rear.

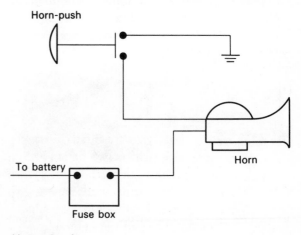

Horn circuit

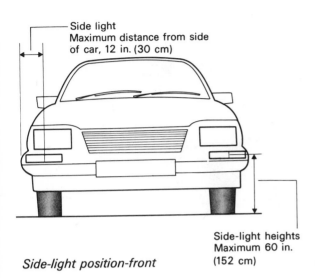

Side light
Maximum distance from side
of car, 12 in. (30 cm)

Side-light heights
Maximum 60 in.
(152 cm)

Side-light position-front

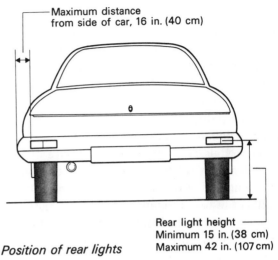

Maximum distance
from side of car, 16 in. (40 cm)

Rear light height
Minimum 15 in. (38 cm)
Maximum 42 in. (107 cm)

Position of rear lights

However, some countries have amber lights to the front. Such lights, whether they be amber, white or red, are called *side-lights*. Their purpose is to show the size and the position of the vehicle. The colour identifies the front and rear of the vehicle. As an extra aid to identification, vehicles are also fitted with red reflectors at the rear. These reflect the lights from other vehicles.

The position of the side-lights is controlled by law. The diagrams show the positions required in the UK. The principle behind this is that the lights are at a nominal height and near to the outside of the vehicle. This gives an indication of the size of the vehicle to other road-users.

Headlights

So that the driver can see on unlit roads and so that the other traffic can clearly see oncoming traffic, headlights are fitted. These are fitted as either one pair or two pairs. The position of the headlights is controlled by law. They are normally fitted with twin-filament bulbs to give dipped and main-beam positions. The dipped position is when the light shines lower to prevent dazzling oncoming traffic and

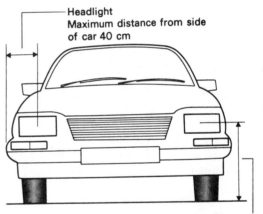

Headlight
Maximum distance from side
of car 40 cm

Headlights height Maximum 42 in. (106 cm)
Minimum 24 in. (61 cm)

Headlight position

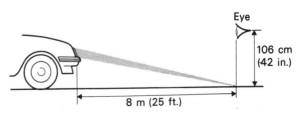

Eye

106 cm
(42 in.)

8 m (25 ft.)

Anti-dazzle regulations

at the same time lights up the road just in front of the vehicle. Even when on main beam, the lights must be set so that they do not dazzle someone 8 m (25 ft) in front of the lights with an eye-level of 106 cm (3 ft 6 in.).

Flasher lights

Flasher lights, or indicators, are fitted to warn other road-users of any intended change of direction. These are generally amber on both the front and rear. When turning right or pulling out to the right the right-hand flasher is operated; the left-hand flasher is used for similar movements to the left. The lights are made to flash by means of a flasher unit.

Flasher unit

Bulbs

The bulb lights up from the glow of the hot filament. In conventional bulbs this is a fine piece of tungsten steel wire heated up until it glows white-hot. The cross-section of a simple single filament bulb is shown in the diagram. As can be seen, it consists of a brass cap, a glass envelope enclosing the filament and two lead connections. The whole assembly is bound together with bitumen or a similar insulating material.

The bulb-fitting may take the form of a screw (an Edison screw as it is called, after the inventor of the bulb) or two bayonets or spigots on the side of the cap. This latter is referred to as a bayonet cap.

Bulbs for headlights and specialist applications such as stop tail lights have two filaments. So that the filaments are correctly aligned when the bulb is in position the bayonets are fitted offset. These are referred to as offset bayonet caps.

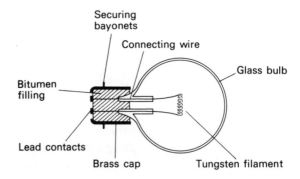

Twin-contact bayonet cap bulb

Light units

The bulb and the reflector are sometimes incorporated into one item, called a *light unit*. The reflector and the glass are equivalent to a

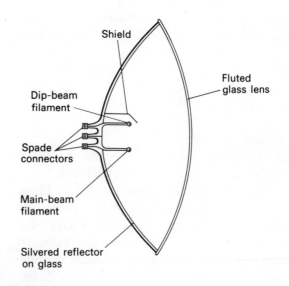

Light unit

glass bulb and cap of a conventional bulb. The filament is connected in the normal way. The light unit has the advantages of having one layer of glass which means that it gives more light. The reflector is sealed so that it cannot rust and the filament is firmly placed to keep in focus. Although they are cheaper to make than separate bulb and reflector units, replacement is expensive as the complete unit must be renewed when faulty.

Spot and fog lights

Spot and fog auxiliary lights are fitted for specialist uses, and the beams given by these lights are shown. The spot light gives a long pencil beam, which is used to spot things a long way away, such as when driving down long straight roads. The fog lamp gives a wide flat beam which is designed to light up a wide area near to the front of the car. This is useful in foggy weather or heavy snow or rain, when visibility is restricted.

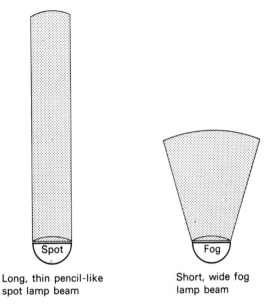

Long, thin pencil-like spot lamp beam

Short, wide fog lamp beam

Spot and fog lamp beams

Wiring diagrams

Side-lights

The side-lights are wired to one switch so that they all come on when the switch is operated. The rear number-plate light is also connected to the side-light system.

Headlights

The headlight switch is combined with the side-light switch in the lighting circuit. The headlights can only be switched on when the side-lights are on. This is to ensure that the red lights are on at the rear of the vehicle. The choice of main beam or dipped beam is made by the dip switch, which may be operated by the hand or the foot.

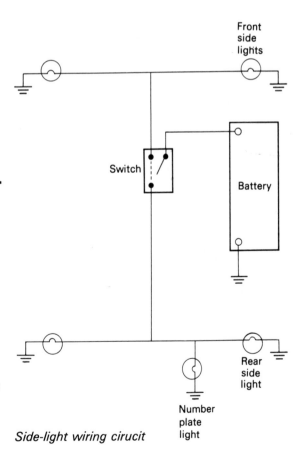

Side-light wiring cirucit

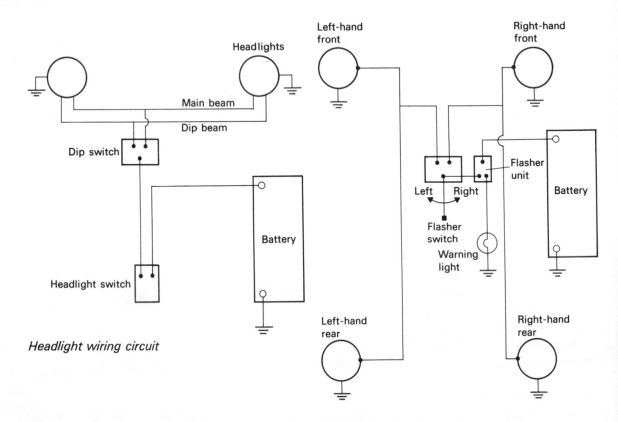

Headlights

Main beam

Dip beam

Dip switch

Battery

Headlight switch

Headlight wiring circuit

Left-hand front

Right-hand front

Flasher unit

Left   Right

Battery

Flasher switch

Warning light

Left-hand rear

Right-hand rear

Flasher circuit

Indicators

The flasher wiring diagram is shown. The choice of left-hand or right-hand flasher is made by a hand-operated switch near the steering wheel. Depending upon the type of car, this is usually a stalk attached to the steering column.

Spot and fog lights

Spot lights and fog lights are simply wired up with separate switches. They are sometimes wired up so that they can only be operated when the headlights are switched on.

Cable

The cable used for wiring is identified in three ways:

1 Type of covering.
2 Number of wire strands.
3 Diameter of each wire strand.

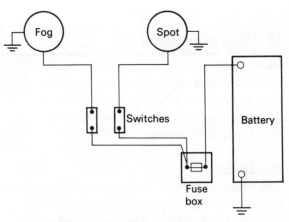

Fog

Spot

Switches

Battery

Fuse box

Spot and fog lamp wiring cirucit

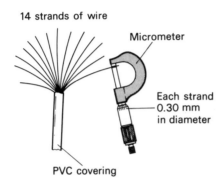

Cable sizes

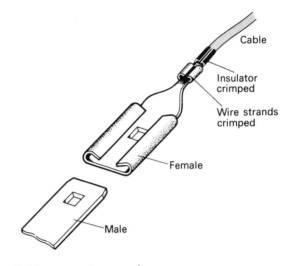

Cable connector: spade

The type of covering is generally PVC, although rubber or woven cotton are used sometimes. A typical number and diameter of wire strands would be denoted as: 14/0.30. In this case, the cable has 14 strands of wire, each being 0.30 mm in diameter. (The diameter can also be given in inches.)

Cable connectors
Several types of connectors are used to connect the cables together or to connect the cables to components. Illustrated are some of the common types. The *spade terminal* has the advantage of being easily pulled on and off. Two sizes of spade terminals are in common use. The *bullet terminal*, like the other two, takes its name from its shape. The bullet-shaped end fits onto the wire. Rubber-covered tubes are used to connect the bullets, one at each end. Connectors are also made to take up to eight bullets. The *eyelet terminal* is used with screws to connect wires to components securely.

Battery terminals
To connect the battery cables to the battery, special terminals are used. Battery terminals are standard sizes. The positive terminal is slightly larger than the negative terminal to prevent them being wrongly connected.

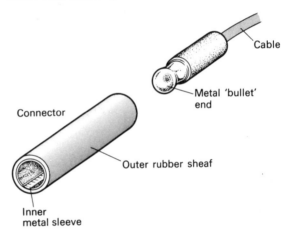

Cable connector: bullet

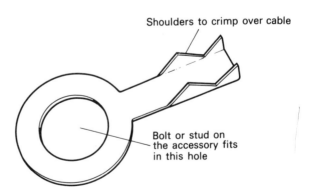

Cable connector: eyelet

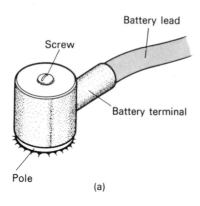

Battery connector. (a) Screw type; (b) clamp type

Positive is identified by either a plus sign(+) or a brown or red colour, the negative with a minus sign(−) or a blue or black colour.

Wiring diagram
A complete wiring diagram is shown. See if you can identify the separate circuits. The diagram shows the electrical wiring system for the Mini Metro. It is reproduced courtesy of the Austin Rover Group.

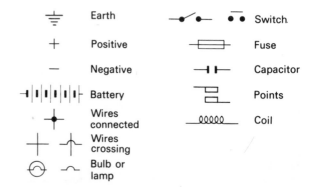

Wiring diagram symbols

The cable colour code is as follows:

B	Black	**P**	Purple
G	Green	**R**	Red
K	Pink	**S**	Slate
LG	Light green	**U**	Blue
N	Brown	**W**	White
O	Orange	**Y**	Yellow

Key to symbols
1 When fitted
2 Connector
3 Instrument printed circuit connector
4 Fuse board printed circuit connector
5 Sealed joint
6 Instrument printed circuit
7 Fuse board printed circuit
8 Component earthed through fixings
9 Component earthed with cable

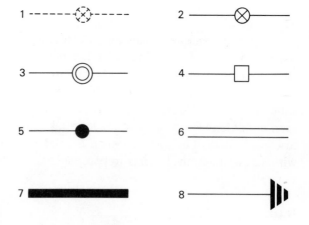

Symbols used in circuit diagram

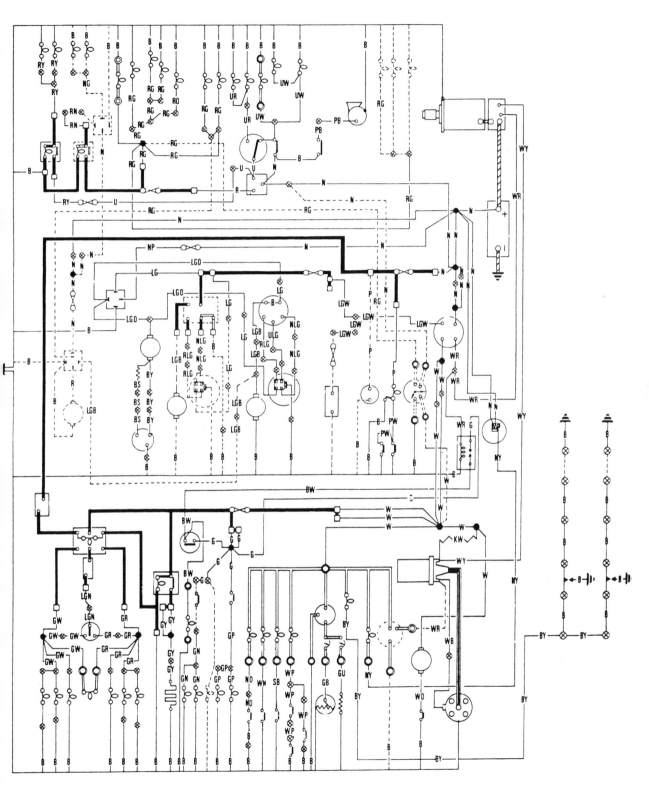

Car wiring diagram

Multiple-choice questions

1 The component which spins the engine over so that it will start is the:
(a) alternator
(b) starter motor
(c) dynamo
(d) ignition key

2 In relation to electric cable, the figures 14/0.30 refer to:
(a) the number of strands and diameter of each strand
(b) length and width
(c) amperage and size
(d) length of cable on a roll

3 Which part of the battery is made from lead peroxide:
(a) the filling of the negative plate
(b) casing
(c) terminals
(d) the filling of the positive plate

4 The component which keeps the battery fully charged is the:
(a) generator
(b) starter motor
(c) coil
(d) distributor

5 When topping up a battery you should always use:
(a) rain water
(b) distilled water
(c) tap water
(d) clean water

6 Spot-lamp beams are identified by their shape, which is:
(a) wide
(b) triangular
(c) flat
(d) narrow

7 *Spade*, *eyelet* and *bullet* are all types of:
(a) alternator
(b) cable connector
(c) battery
(d) lamp bulb

8 The level of electrolyte in the battery should be checked at least:
(a) once a month
(b) once a week
(c) once a year
(d) once a day

9 Each cell of a battery gives:
(a) 6V
(b) 3V
(c) 2V
(d) 12V

10 Dead flat on the hydrometer scale is:
(a) 1.200
(b) 1.100
(c) 1.300
(d) 1.000

14 Safety

Various aspects of safety and the vehicle have been discussed under the relevant headings. In this chapter we are going to discuss safety in general terms with particular reference to workshop equipment.

Dress

The normal dress for a mechanic is a boiler suit. This should be free from loose and ragged edges. The cuffs and collar should be buttoned, the arms and legs should be close-fitting. Shoes should be tough, with thick soles to prevent penetration by sharp objects. The toecaps should be reinforced to prevent the toes being crushed if something heavy is dropped on them.

Electrical plugs

The diagram shows the correct way to wire up a three-pin plug according to the regulations of the International Standards Organisation. The live wire is brown, the neutral is blue and the earth is green and yellow. Sockets must not be overloaded by fitting more than one plug into them. The plug must be fitted with the correct amperage of fuse for the item being used. The wires should be firmly fitted and there should be no stray pieces in the plug.

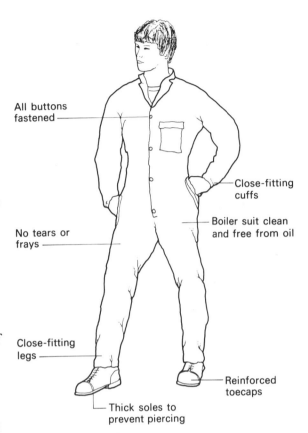

Mechanic's dress

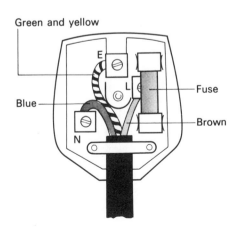

Three-pin plug

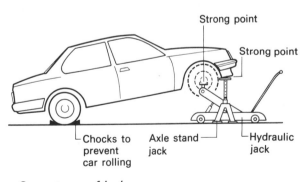

Correct use of jacks

Jack

When jacking up a car a strong point should be chosen. The wheels, which remain on the road, must be chocked to prevent the car rolling away. The end of the car which is raised must be supported on axle stands. Never go under the car unless it is firmly supported on these.

Hoist

There are two main types of hoists, or ramps as they are sometimes called: those supported by oil pressure and those using screwed poles. The diagram shows a hoist and indicates the areas to be checked when using it, i.e. the end stops must be up. One end stop is automatic, and works as soon as the hoist is raised from the ground. Chocks must be used to hold the vehicle in place when it is on the hoist.

Care must be taken when working with vehicles raised on the hoist. Tools must be placed securely to prevent them falling. Never walk or work under a hoist when someone is working above it.

Pit

An alternative to the hoist is the pit, i.e. a hole dug into the ground to gain access to the underside of the vehicle. The floor must be kept free of oil, grease and other liquids to prevent the possibility of slipping. The exit stairs or ladder must be kept clear for easy escape in an emergency. The top must be boarded when not in use. An extractor fan can be used to clear fumes from the pit.

Compressed air

The diagram shows a typical air-line arrangement. The condition of the metal lines, the rubber lines and the connectors must be checked for damage. The pressure gauge must be checked at frequent intervals to ensure that the compressor tank is not run at over-high pressure. Compressor pressure is automatically controlled, so if the pressure becomes too high, switch off at the main isolator switch and seek help from the foreman.

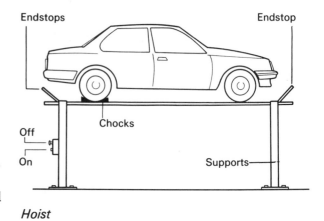

Hoist

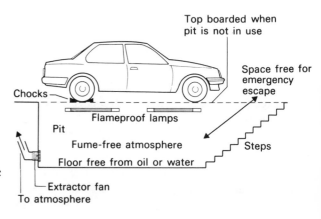

Pit

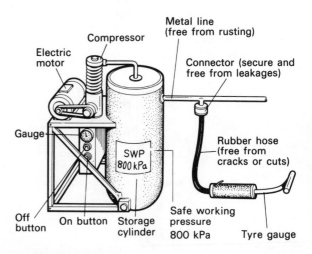

Air-line arrangement

Any other visible faults must be reported. The compressor should be serviced by specialist staff, as it requires specialist knowledge and care.

Electric drill

The electric drill is one of the most frequently used power tools. It must be checked for damage to its casing and to ensure that the chuck is not loose. The cable must not be frayed or contaminated with oil. The plug fuse must also be of the correct rating.

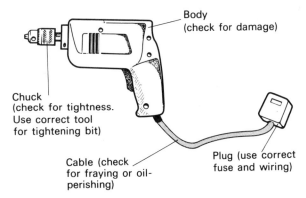

Body (check for damage)

Chuck (check for tightness. Use correct tool for tightening bit)

Cable (check for fraying or oil-perishing)

Plug (use correct fuse and wiring)

Electric drill

Multiple-choice questions

1 Before using an electric drill you should check the condition of the:
  (a) hole
  (b) size
  (c) paintwork
  (d) casing

2 The live wire on a three pin plug is coloured:
  (a) red
  (b) blue
  (c) brown
  (d) green and yellow

3 It is essential that a pit has:
  (a) an easy to use, unobstructed exit
  (b) a supply of running water
  (c) concrete walls
  (d) a polished floor surface

4 The pressure in a compressor tank must not exceed:
  (a) 100 psi
  (b) 10 bar
  (c) the figure stated by the manufacturer
  (d) 5 kPa

5 You should never work under a car unless the end which is raised is supported by:
  (a) bricks
  (b) a jack
  (c) a rope
  (d) axle stands

6 Mechanics' shoes should be tough with thick soles to prevent:
  (a) frostbite in the winter
  (b) penetration by sharp objects
  (c) oil penetration
  (d) blisters

7 The normal dress for a mechanic is:
  (a) a close fitting boiler suit
  (b) a loose fitting boiler suit
  (c) an oil-proof jacket
  (d) a smock

8 To hold a vehicle in place on a hoist you should use:
  (a) the handbrake
  (b) a hammer
  (c) fingers
  (d) chocks

9   The fuse in a three-pin plug is:
    (a) coloured brown
    (b) fitted to the positive pin
    (c) fitted to earth
    (d) attached to the blue wire

10 When not in use, the top of the pit should be:
    (a) oiled
    (b) well lit
    (c) boarded over
    (d) covered with a tarpaulin

Answers to multiple-choice questions

Question	1	2	3	4	5	6	7	8	9	10
Chapter										
1	c	b	d	b	c	a	b	a	c	a
2	b	a	c	d	b	a	b	c	b	d
3	d	a	a	d	b	c	c	a	b	d
4	b	a	b	d	b	a	c	c	d	a
5	d	c	a	b	d	b	c	a	b	b
6	b	c	d	a	a	d	a	b	d	c
7	b	c	b	a	b	d	b	a	c	b
8	c	a	c	d	a	c	b	d	a	c
9	c	a	a	d	a	d	c	a	b	d
10	b	d	c	a	a	b	d	a	c	c
11	a	d	b	c	a	b	d	b	a	c
12	b	c	d	a	c	a	c	b	a	b
13	b	a	d	a	b	d	b	a	c	b
14	c	c	a	c	d	b	a	d	b	c

Index